# Target
## Get back on track

**GRADE 5**

## Edexcel GCSE (9-1)
# English Language
# Writing

## David Grant

New College
New College Drive
Swindon
SN3 1AH
www.newcollege.ac.uk
01793 611470

D1344801

# Contents

This workbook has been developed using the Pearson Progression Map and Scale for English.

To find out more about the Progression Scale for English and to see how it relates to indicative GCSE 9–1 grades go to www.pearsonschools.co.uk/ProgressionServices

**Helping you to formulate grade predictions, apply interventions and track progress.**

Any reference to indicative grades in the Pearson Target Workbooks and Pearson Progression Services is not to be used as an accurate indicator of how a student will be awarded a grade for their GCSE exams.

You have told us that mapping the Steps from the Pearson Progression Maps to indicative grades will make it simpler for you to accumulate the evidence to formulate your own grade predictions, apply any interventions and track student progress. We're really excited about this work and its potential for helping teachers and students. It is, however, important to understand that this mapping is for guidance only to support teachers' own predictions of progress and is not an accurate predictor of grades.

Our Pearson Progression Scale is criterion referenced. If a student can perform a task or demonstrate a skill, we say they are working at a certain Step according to the criteria. Teachers can mark assessments and issue results with reference to these criteria which do not depend on the wider cohort in any given year. For GCSE exams however, all Awarding Organisations set the grade boundaries with reference to the strength of the cohort in any given year. For more information about how this works please visit: https://qualifications.pearson.com/en/support/support-topics/results-certification/understanding-marks-and-grades.html/Teacher

# ① Generating ideas for imaginative writing

This unit will help you generate ideas for an imaginative writing task. The skills you will build are to:

- respond to the task and develop some initial ideas
- use a story structure to develop your ideas further
- explore ways to make the story you are planning more engaging and interesting.

In the exam, you will be asked to tackle an imaginative writing task such as the one below. This unit will prepare you to plan your own response to this question.

**Exam-style question**

Look at the images provided.

Write about a time when you, or someone you know, experienced a surprise.

Your response could be real or imagined. You may wish to base your response on one of the images.

(40 marks)

The three key questions in the **skills boosts** will help you prepare your response.

**1** How do I begin to generate ideas?

**2** What do I need in order to complete a successful story plan?

**3** How do I develop my ideas to engage the reader?

Look at one student's story plan on the next page. It was written in response to the task above.

**Exam-style question**

Write a story about a time when you experienced a surprise.

| | |
|---|---|
| 1. I woke up in the night. | Cold, dark, sleepy. Curtain flapping in cold breeze. Feeling frightened. |
| 2. I heard strange noises coming from downstairs. | I hear a strange noise. Sit up suddenly. Listen. I can hear thumping noises. Don't know what to do. Think about waking mum up or calling the police. Decide to be brave. Not sure why! |
| 3. Terrified, I went downstairs to see what it was. | Build tension here. Darkness. Heart beating. Feet creaking on stairs. Freeze! Imagining all the things it could be: ghost, burglar, or worse. |
| 4. It was my sister sleepwalking. | Build tension even more. Crashing, banging coming from front room. Hand shaking on door handle. Open the door to see shadowy figure. It stops moving and turns to look at me... It's my sister. |

(1) Look carefully at the story plan above. Note down ✎ at least **three** ways in which the writer is trying to engage and entertain the reader with their story.

.......................................................................................................

.......................................................................................................

.......................................................................................................

.......................................................................................................

.......................................................................................................

.......................................................................................................

.......................................................................................................

(2) Can you think of any ideas that might make this story even more engaging or entertaining? Note ✎ your suggestions below.

.......................................................................................................

.......................................................................................................

.......................................................................................................

.......................................................................................................

.......................................................................................................

.......................................................................................................

.......................................................................................................

.......................................................................................................

# 1 How do I begin to generate ideas?

One way to begin planning an imaginative writing task is to focus on the key event or idea in the task and ask yourself questions to help you generate and develop ideas.

**(1)** Look again at the exam-style question from page 1. Circle Ⓐ the key idea in the task.

**Exam-style question**

Write about a time when you, or someone you know, experienced a surprise.

**(2)** Ask yourself questions about the key idea you have identified.

> **?** What could this event be?

> **?** Will it be a positive or a negative experience?

> **?** What will be the narrator's role in this event?

Note 🖉 your first ideas in the space below:

**(3)** Look at the images provided in the exam-style question to help you to generate and develop your ideas. Note 🖉 your ideas in the space below.

|  |  |
|---|---|
| What are they looking at on the phone? A message? What does it say? A picture? Of what or who? Who posted it? Why? Who are the people looking at the phone? You? Your friends? | What's in the box? Who is he? You? A relative? Who gave him the present? He looks pleased... how will he react when he opens it? |
| | |

## ② What do I need in order to complete a successful story plan?

When you have generated some ideas, it can be helpful to think about the ingredients you need for a **complete** story. One way to approach this is to think about story structure.

| 1. The exposition | 2. The conflict | 3. The climax | 4. The resolution |
|---|---|---|---|
| Introduces the characters and their situation. | There is a problem. | The problem worsens. | The problem is resolved – but not always happily. |

For example, in the student's plan on page 2, the four stages are the following.

| I woke up in the night. | I heard strange noises coming from downstairs. | Terrified, I went downstairs to see what it was. | It was my sister sleepwalking. |
|---|---|---|---|

① Think about the key idea in the writing task.

**Exam-style question**

Write about a time when you, or someone you know, experienced a surprise.

Where in the story will this key idea occur?

**?** If it is a nasty surprise, it could be the **conflict** of your story.

**?** If it is a nice surprise, it could happen in the **exposition** of your story – a nice surprise that sparks a problem and leads to its resolution.

**?** Or the nice surprise could form the **resolution** of your story – the thing that resolves the conflict in your story.

Add ✏ your ideas so far to the appropriate box of the planning table below.

| 1. The exposition | 2. The conflict | 3. The climax | 4. The resolution |
|---|---|---|---|
|  |  |  |  |

② Look at your story plan so far. Are there any gaps in your plan? For example:
- if you have completed the **resolution** box, what **conflict** and **climax** could build up to this?
- if you have completed the **conflict** box, how could the situation worsen to create a **climax** which can then be resolved in the **resolution**?

③ Your **first** ideas are not always your **best** ideas. Look again at the planning table above. Can you add ✏ to, improve, or change any of your ideas to create a better story?

## 3 How do I develop my ideas to engage the reader?

When you have completed your plan, you can further develop it to:

* make it an original story (beware of copying ideas from films or stories you have read!)
* make it a more interesting, engaging story.

Look at one student's plan for the exam-style question that you looked at on page 1.

| Exposition | Conflict | Climax | Resolution |
| --- | --- | --- | --- |
| I'm upset because no one is bothered about my birthday. | I get a text from my boyfriend. He wants me to meet him. | I tell my friend. She says he might want to dump me. | I go to his house. He's arranged a surprise birthday party for me. |

Think about how this student could add some of these ideas to develop their planning.

① Writers often create **heroes and villains** in their stories to manipulate the reader's response – readers want the hero to triumph and the villain to fail.

    **a** Who is the hero of this story? How could the hero be made even more **heroic**? ✎

..................................................................................................................................................................

    **b** Who could be the villain in this story? How could this villain be made even more **villainous**? ✎

..................................................................................................................................................................

..................................................................................................................................................................

..................................................................................................................................................................

..................................................................................................................................................................

..................................................................................................................................................................

② Writers create **mystery and suspense** by withholding information, encouraging the reader to ask questions. Do any of the elements of the story plan above suggest mystery? How could you add mystery and create suspense? ✎

..................................................................................................................................................................

..................................................................................................................................................................

③ Writers use **tension** to build suspense before the mystery is revealed. How could you add tension to the story plan above? ✎

..................................................................................................................................................................

..................................................................................................................................................................

④ Everyone loves a **happy ending** – but sometimes they can be too sickly and sentimental. How could the ending in the story plan above be made: ✎

    **a** bitter-sweet ..........................................................................................................................................

..................................................................................................................................................................

    **b** tragically sad? ....................................................................................................................................

..................................................................................................................................................................

# Sample response

To plan an effective narrative writing task, you need to:

- focus on the key idea in the task
- gather some initial ideas thinking about this key event and the narrator's role in it
- develop your ideas using the exposition–conflict–climax–resolution structure
- develop your ideas further, thinking about heroes and villains, suspense and tension, happy and unhappy endings.

Look at this exam-style writing task, which you saw at the start of the unit.

**Exam-style question**

Look at the images provided.

Write about a time when you, or someone you know, experienced a surprise.

Your response could be real or imagined. You may wish to base your response on one of the images.

(40 marks)

Then look at this student's plan for the task.

- My mum told me that we were going to visit my auntie and my cousins who live in Manchester.

- We got in the car and we ended up at an airport.

- My mum said 'Surprise!' and explained that we were going to Disneyland Paris and were meeting my auntie and cousins there.

How could this student's ideas be developed? Add 🖉 your ideas to the plan above.

# Your turn!

You are now going to **plan** your response to this exam-style task.

**Exam-style question**

Look at the images provided.

Write about a time when you, or someone you know, experienced a surprise.

Your response could be real or imagined. You may wish to base your response on one of the images.

(40 marks)

**1** Note 🖉 down **three** different story ideas that you might use in response to this task. Aim to sum up each idea in just one sentence.

Story idea 1 ..................................................................................................................................................

....................................................................................................................................................................

....................................................................................................................................................................

....................................................................................................................................................................

Story idea 2 ..................................................................................................................................................

....................................................................................................................................................................

....................................................................................................................................................................

....................................................................................................................................................................

Story idea 3 ..................................................................................................................................................

....................................................................................................................................................................

....................................................................................................................................................................

....................................................................................................................................................................

**2** Which of your ideas could, when developed, make the most engaging, entertaining story? Write 🖉 a sentence or two explaining your answer.

....................................................................................................................................................................

....................................................................................................................................................................

....................................................................................................................................................................

**3** Now **plan** 🖉 your response to the above exam-style question on paper.

**Unit 1 Generating ideas – imaginative writing**    **7**

# Review your skills

## Check up

Review your response to the exam-style question on page 7. Tick ⊘ the column to show how well you think you have done each of the following.

| | Not quite ⊘ | Nearly there ⊘ | Got it! ⊘ |
|---|---|---|---|
| developed an initial idea | ☐ | ☐ | ☐ |
| used story structure to develop the idea | ☐ | ☐ | ☐ |
| developed the idea further to engage the reader | ☐ | ☐ | ☐ |

Look over all your work in this unit.

Note 🖉 down the three most important things to remember when planning an imaginative writing task.

1. ............................................................................................................
   ............................................................................................................

2. ............................................................................................................
   ............................................................................................................

3. ............................................................................................................
   ............................................................................................................

## Need more practice?

Plan your response to the exam-style question below.

**Exam-style question**

Write about an experience in which honesty and/or dishonesty played an important role.

Your response could be real or imagined.

(40 marks)

How confident do you feel about each of these **skills?** Colour 🖉 in the bars.

**1** How do I begin to generate ideas?

**2** What do I need in order to complete a successful story plan?

**3** How do I develop my ideas to engage the reader?

# ② Generating ideas – transactional writing

This unit will help you learn how to generate ideas for a transactional writing task. The skills you will build are to:

- identify and clarify your point of view

- develop key points to convey your point of view

- support your key points with evidence.

In the exam, you will be asked to tackle writing tasks such as the one below. This unit will prepare you to write your own response to this question.

---

**Exam-style question**

Write the text for a speech giving your views on health and fitness.
In your speech you could write about:

- why health and fitness is important
- whether people should do more to keep healthy and fit
- ways in which people can keep healthy and fit
  as well was any other ideas you might have.

(40 marks)

---

The three key questions in the **skills boosts** will help you generate ideas for transactional writing tasks.

① **How do I make my point?**    ② **How do I develop my ideas?**    ③ **How do I support my ideas?**

Look at one student's plan on the next page.

|   |   |   |
|---|---|---|
| ☐ | Being unfit and unhealthy can lead to lots of health problems. | Obesity, heart attacks, diabetes, dying young. Costs a fortune to look after them when they get older and get ill. |
| ☐ | People's behaviour makes them fit and unhealthy. | Lying around in bed or on settee, eating a packet of biscuits, watching telly, playing computer games, online shopping, smoking, drinking... |
| ☐ | You don't have to be an Olympic athlete to be fit and healthy. Everyone can do it. | You can walk, don't get a lift. Stop eating sweets, cakes and biscuits so often. Cut out fizzy drinks. Think about what, and how much, you eat. |
| ☐ | Getting fit and healthy can be fun. | Go running or take up a sport with friends... walk the dog, walk to school. Ditch the dodgy burger and cook something delicious. |
| ☐ | Get fitter and healthier. You'll feel better, look better and **be** better. |   |

(1) What's this student's point of view? Summarise ✎ it in a sentence or two.

.......................................................................................................................................................

.......................................................................................................................................................

.......................................................................................................................................................

.......................................................................................................................................................

.......................................................................................................................................................

.......................................................................................................................................................

(2) Look carefully at each point this student uses to get their views across.

(a) Which point gets this student's views across most powerfully? Tick it. ✓

(b) Write ✎ a sentence or two explaining your choice.

.......................................................................................................................................................

.......................................................................................................................................................

.......................................................................................................................................................

.......................................................................................................................................................

(c) Which of this student's points is the weakest? Cross it. ✗

(d) Write ✎ a sentence or two explaining your choice.

.......................................................................................................................................................

.......................................................................................................................................................

.......................................................................................................................................................

.......................................................................................................................................................

# 1 How do I make my point?

Before you can generate ideas for your writing, you need to decide on your point of view.

Look again at the exam-style question from page 9.

**Exam-style question**

Write the text for a speech giving your views on health and fitness.

**(1)** To help you develop your point of view on health and fitness, think about all of the different ideas that come to mind when you think about this topic. Add  at least **four** ideas to the spidergram below.

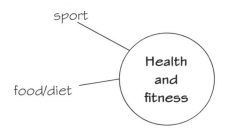

**(2)** Now think about some other people's views on health and fitness. Which of the following points of view do you agree with **most strongly**? Tick one. ✓

☐ **?** People forget about health and fitness. They need to be reminded how important it is or they won't do anything about it.

☐ **?** Life's too short to be worried about health and fitness. You should just enjoy yourself and hope for the best.

☐ **?** People spend too much time worrying about health and fitness. Most people are healthy and fit already.

☐ **?** Health and fitness are important but it doesn't mean you have to worry about them all the time.

☐ **?** Health and fitness are the most important things in life. If you haven't got your health, you've got nothing.

**(3)** Finally, think about **your** point of view. What are **your** views on health and fitness? Write  a sentence or two summing them up.

...........................................................................................................

...........................................................................................................

...........................................................................................................

...........................................................................................................

## 2 How do I develop my ideas?

When you write to express your views, you are aiming to influence your readers' views so that they agree with you. To achieve this, you can point out:

- the benefits of your point of view – why your point of view can improve things
- the problems that could be solved if everyone shared your views.

(1) Look again at the exam-style question from page 9.

**Exam-style question**

Write the text for a speech giving your views on health and fitness.

(a) Think about your views on health and fitness. What are the **benefits** of your point of view? How would things be better if everyone agreed with you? Note down 🖉 at least **three** ideas.

........................................................................................................

........................................................................................................

........................................................................................................

(b) What are the **problems** that your point of view can help with? You could think about:

- people who are not concerned about health and fitness
- people who are too concerned about health and fitness
- things that prevent people being healthy and fit
- things that prevent people wanting to be healthy and fit.

Note down 🖉 **three** problems that you might want to write about in your response to the exam-style question above. For each problem, note down 🖉 one or two possible solutions.

| Problems | | Solutions | |
|---|---|---|---|
| | → | | |
| | → | | |
| | → | | |

(2) Look again at the benefits, problems and solutions you have identified above. Which of these ideas is most likely to influence your readers? Tick ✓ any that you think are strong enough to be included in your response to the exam-style question above. Cross ✗ any that are not.

# 3 How do I support my ideas?

The most effective way to convince people that they should agree with your point of view is to give evidence that proves its value. Evidence can be:

- a fact or statistic
- an expert's point of view
- an example from your own experience.

It can be difficult to use experts' points of view or precise statistics in an exam as you are not able to look them up or check them. You can, however, refer to generally accepted facts such as the following as evidence.

**A.** Obesity has been a growing problem for several years in the UK.

**B.** Soft drinks often contain huge amounts of sugar.

**C.** Surveys frequently show that a significant number of people take little or no exercise.

**D.** Research has shown that taking some exercise every day can make a big difference to your health and fitness.

(1) Now look at these key points. Which piece of evidence, A, B, C or D, best supports each one? Add the letter of your chosen evidence to the table below.

| Key points | Evidence |
|---|---|
| 1. Being unfit and unhealthy can lead to lots of health problems. | |
| 2. You don't have to be an Olympic athlete to be healthy and fit. Everyone can do it. | |
| 3. People's behaviour makes them unfit and unhealthy. | |

(2) Now look at this key point: | Getting fit and healthy can be fun. |

Write a sentence or two, giving an example from your own experience as evidence to support it. You could write about:

- an example of a healthy eating choice you make **or** an example of exercise you take **and**
- the impact it has had on your life.

......................................................................................................................

......................................................................................................................

......................................................................................................................

......................................................................................................................

......................................................................................................................

......................................................................................................................

# Sample response

To generate ideas when you are writing to present a viewpoint, you need to:

- decide on your point of view
- develop your point of view with benefits and solutions to problems that your ideas will bring
- identify evidence to support your ideas.

Now look again at the exam-style writing task that you saw at the start of the unit.

**Exam-style question**

Write the text for a speech giving your views on health and fitness.
In your speech you could write about:

- why health and fitness is important
- whether people should do more to keep healthy and fit
- ways in which people can keep healthy and fit
  as well was any other ideas you might have.

(40 marks)

Look at this student's planning for the task.

*My view:* We worry *too much* about health and fitness. We can live our lives **and** live longer.

*Points*

1. Some people become obsessed with going to the gym and don't have time for anything else.

2. Exercise isn't always good for you. You can damage yourself permanently by doing too much exercise.

3. It's important not to eat too much and to have some exercise, but you need to get the balance right.

*Evidence*

A friend goes to the gym every evening. I hardly ever see him.

My mum used to do a lot of running but had to stop because she's damaged her knees.

Research shows that lots of things can make you healthier: laughing, spending time with friends and family, and even having a pet!

[ benefits ]     [ problems ]     [ solutions ]

Find each of the benefits, problems and solutions in the student's plan.

Underline (A) and label (✏) at least one of each in the text.

# Your turn!

You are now going to plan your response to this exam-style task.

**Exam-style question**

Write the text for a speech giving your views on health and fitness.
In your speech you could write about:

- why health and fitness is important
- whether people should do more to keep healthy and fit
- ways in which people can keep healthy and fit
  as well was any other ideas you might have.

(40 marks)

**1** What will be the main point of view that you want to get across in your speech?
Write 🖉 a sentence or two summarising it.

..................................................................................................................................

..................................................................................................................................

..................................................................................................................................

**2** What benefits, problems and solutions will you talk about in your speech? Note 🖉 them below.

The problems we face are...

The solutions I'm suggesting are...

The benefits of my ideas about health and fitness are that...

**3** Now plan 🖉 your response to the above exam-style question on paper.

# Review your skills

## Check up

Review your response to the exam-style question on page 15. Tick ✓ the column to show how well you think you have done each of the following.

|  | Not quite ✓ | Nearly there ✓ | Got it! ✓ |
|---|---|---|---|
| identified my point of view | ☐ | ☐ | ☐ |
| developed key points | ☐ | ☐ | ☐ |
| supported key points with evidence | ☐ | ☐ | ☐ |

Look over all your work in this unit.

Note down 🖉 the three most important things to remember when generating ideas for transactional writing.

1. ........................................................................

........................................................................

2. ........................................................................

........................................................................

3. ........................................................................

........................................................................

## Need more practice?

Plan your response to the task below.

### Exam-style question

Write an article for a newspaper giving your views on the impact that technology has on our lives.

In your article you could write about:

- the ways in which we use technology
- how technology can solve problems and create problems
- whether we rely on technology too much as well as any other ideas you might have. **(40 marks)**

How confident do you feel about each of these **skills?** Colour 🖉 in the bars.

**1** How do I make my point?

**2** How do I develop my ideas?

**3** How do I support my ideas?

# ③ Structuring your ideas – imaginative writing

This unit will help you learn how to structure your ideas for an imaginative writing task. The skills you will build are to:

- plan a satisfying ending to your imaginative writing
- create an engaging opening to your imaginative writing
- manipulate your story structure to create impact.

In the exam, you will be asked to tackle writing tasks such as the one below. This unit will prepare you to write your own response to this question.

**Exam-style question**

Write about a time when you, or someone you know, got into trouble.

Your response could be real or imagined.     **(40 marks)**

The three key questions in the **skills boosts** will help you to structure your ideas for an imaginative writing task.

① **How do I create a satisfying ending?** > ② **How do I engage my readers from the very beginning?** > ③ **How can I structure my writing for impact?**

Look at one student's plan on the next page.

- My friend came round when my mum was out at work. She ate my mum's dinner and said we should go out. I agreed.

- My friend persuaded me to borrow my mum's best necklace. I said I should ask my mum. My friend said my mum would never notice. So I agreed.

- We went out – and I lost the necklace.

- My friend persuaded me not to tell my mum. So I agreed.

- A week later, I saw my friend in town. She was wearing my mum's necklace.

- She said she had just found it and was going to bring it back to me the next day.

- I made her give it back there and then.

- I realised that I should never have listened to her and not been such a doormat. I never spoke to her again.

**1** Think about:

- the way this story begins, develops and ends

- the characters and how they develop.

**a** What is effective about this story plan? Note your thoughts below.

**b** What could be improved in this story plan? Note your thoughts below.

| What is effective? 🖉 | What could be improved? 🖉 |
| --- | --- |
| | |

**How do I create a satisfying ending?**

The ending, or resolution, of a narrative text should resolve the conflict established in the story. However, the ways in which **events** or **characters develop** in the ending of the story can make it much more satisfying for your reader.

> For more help with story structure, see *Unit 1*.

① One way to make a story ending more satisfying is to show the impact that the events in the story have on the central character, or characters. For example:

The events in the story transform

| | into | |
|---|---|---|
| a mean, angry person | | a caring, generous person. |
| a shy, quiet person | | a person being brave enough to stand up in front of an audience. |
| | | |

Add 🖉 another idea to the table above.

② Look at the story plan below.

| Jimmy has spent all his time and money creating a new invention: a car that runs on water. | → | He gathers the family for the exciting moment when he tests the car. It won't start. He has wasted his time. | → | Jimmy and his family have no money. The children's clothes are full of holes. They are hungry. Bills are piling up. | → | ? |
|---|---|---|---|---|---|---|

Now look at three ways in which events can develop in the ending of the story.

A. The lucky ending: a piece of luck changes everything.

> Luckily, Jimmy finds a bag of money on the pavement and all his problems are solved. ☐

B. The surprise ending: an unexpected event changes everything.

> Jimmy gets a letter. He has inherited a fortune from a long lost uncle. All their problems are solved. ☐

C. The developing ending: events set up earlier in the story develop and change everything.

> Jimmy has one last try at starting the car. It won't start. He loses his temper, throws a hammer at it – and it starts! They're going to be rich! ☐

Which of these three types of ending do you think is most effective and satisfying? Tick ✓ it. Write 🖉 a sentence or two explaining your choice.

.............................................................................................................................

.............................................................................................................................

.............................................................................................................................

③ Think of another satisfying ending for the story above. Sum it up 🖉 in a sentence or two.

.............................................................................................................................

.............................................................................................................................

**Unit 3 Structuring your ideas – imaginative writing** 19

## 2 How do I engage my readers from the very beginning?

An engaging opening is a sure sign of a skilled writer. It makes readers want to read the whole story.

① Look at these four different openings to a spooky ghost story. Each one uses a different technique.

| Introduce the main **character** | Maddy was a fourteen-year-old girl who lived with her mum and three sisters in a small house on a hill in the middle of nowhere. They had two cats and a goldfish called Barney. | ☐ |
|---|---|---|
| Create the mood with **description** | Somewhere in the pitch black darkness of night, someone was screaming but, sitting in their small house in the middle of nowhere, Maddy and her mum heard nothing. | ☐ |
| Grab attention with dramatic **dialogue** | 'What was that?' said Maddy, sitting bolt upright. 'I didn't hear anything,' said her mum, wandering over to the window and peering out into the darkness. | ☐ |
| Jump straight into the **action** | Maddy heard a scream. She ran out of the front door into the night. She peered into the darkness. In the distance, she could just make out a dark shape. It was moving. It was coming towards her. And it was moving fast. | ☐ |

**a** Tick ✓ the openings that are most effective and cross ✗ those that are least effective.

**b** Write ✎ a sentence or two explaining your choices.

.............................................................................................................................

.............................................................................................................................

.............................................................................................................................

.............................................................................................................................

② Look again at the opening of the student's plan for a story about getting into trouble on page 18.

- My friend came round when my mum was out at work. She ate my mum's dinner and said we should go out. I agreed.
- My friend persuaded me to borrow my mum's best necklace. I said I should ask my mum. My friend said my mum would never notice. So I agreed.

Using the techniques that you decided were most effective in question 1, write ✎ an engaging opening to the story. Label ✎ it with the technique you are using, for example, 'dialogue'.

.............................................................................................................................

.............................................................................................................................

.............................................................................................................................

.............................................................................................................................

.............................................................................................................................

## 3 How can I structure my writing for impact?

Stories are usually told **chronologically** – that is, the events in the story unfold in the order in which they take place. However, one way to give the opening and ending of your story extra impact is to tell your story **non-chronologically**.

1. Look at this story plan: it uses the four part story structure, **Exposition–Conflict–Climax–Resolution**.

| A. Exposition | B. Conflict | C. Climax | D. Resolution |
|---|---|---|---|
| Jimmy has spent all his time and money creating a new invention: a car that runs on water. | He gathers the family for the exciting moment when he tests the car. It won't start. He has wasted his time. | Jimmy and his family have no money. The children's clothes are full of holes. They are hungry. Bills are piling up. | Jimmy has one last try at starting the car. It won't start. He loses his temper, throws a hammer at it – and it starts! They're going to be rich! |

Now think about the impact on the reader of opening the story, with:

- either B. **the conflict**

> *Jimmy inserted the ignition key, his fingers fumbling, his whole body trembling. His wife and children stood, nervous and excited, waiting for the engine to leap into life...*

- or C. **the climax**

> *'If you hadn't wasted all your time and money on that stupid car, we wouldn't be in this mess!' shrieked Jimmy' wife. Jimmy stared silently at the floor.*

- or D. **the resolution**

> *Jimmy grabbed a hammer and hurled it at the car. 'You useless pile of junk!' he screamed. The car replied with a roar. The engine had started. Jimmy's jaw dropped.*

...and then going back to A. **the Exposition** to explain how Jimmy's story began.

a. Answer the questions below, circling Ⓐ one or more letters: A, B, C or D.

　i.　Which would be an engaging opening to the story?　　　　A　B　C　D

　ii.　Which would prompt the reader to ask questions?　　　　A　B　C　D

　iii.　Which would spoil the story by revealing events too quickly?　A　B　C　D

b. Write ✏ a sentence or two explaining your choices.

..................................................................................................................................

..................................................................................................................................

..................................................................................................................................

..................................................................................................................................

..................................................................................................................................

**Unit 3 Structuring your ideas – imaginative writing** 　21

# Sample response

To structure imaginative writing effectively, you should consider:

- using a typical story structure, such as **Exposition–Conflict–Climax–Resolution**
- ways to engage your reader from the very opening of the story
- creating a satisfying ending
- telling your story non-chronologically to create additional impact.

Now look at this exam-style writing task, which you saw at the start of the unit.

**Exam-style question**

Write about a time when you, or someone you know, got into trouble.

Your response could be real or imagined.

(40 marks)

(1) Look at this story plan.

| A. Exposition | B. Conflict | C. Climax | D. Resolution |
|---|---|---|---|
| My mum told me to go to the shops and buy something for dinner. | I went to the shops, saw a huge delicious cake and bought it. There was no money left for dinner. | I didn't know what to do. After an hour, I decided to hide the evidence. I ate the cake and felt sick. | I got home. My family were just finishing a delicious smelling takeaway. I was grounded for a week. |

(a) Look carefully at the **Exposition.** Write 🖉 the first sentence or two of the story, aiming to make it as engaging as possible.

.................................................................................................................................

.................................................................................................................................

.................................................................................................................................

(b) Look carefully at the **Resolution.** Can you think of a more satisfying ending to the story? Write 🖉 a sentence or two explaining your ideas.

.................................................................................................................................

.................................................................................................................................

.................................................................................................................................

(c) Could you restructure the story non-chronologically to add more impact? Write 🖉 a sentence or two, explaining your ideas and the impact they might have on the reader.

.................................................................................................................................

.................................................................................................................................

.................................................................................................................................

# Your turn!

You are now going to plan your response to this exam-style task.

**Exam-style question**

Write about a time when you, or someone you know, got into trouble.

Your response could be real or imagined.

(40 marks)

(1) Use the questions below to come up with some initial ideas ✏.

> What kind of trouble were you in?
>
> Whose fault was it – yours or someone else's?
>
> What were the consequences?
>
> How did you try to solve the situation?
>
> Were you successful?

(2) Now develop ✏ your ideas using the Exposition–Conflict–Climax–Resolution structure.

| A. Exposition | B. Conflict | C. Climax | D. Resolution |
|---|---|---|---|
|  |  |  |  |

(3) How will you engage your reader straight away in the opening? Note ✏ your ideas below.

(4) How could you make the ending more satisfying? Note ✏ your ideas.

(5) Now think about the structure of your story. Could you add more impact by structuring it non-chronologically? Note ✏ your ideas below.

(6) Now plan ✏ your response to the exam-style question above on paper.

**Unit 3 Structuring your ideas – imaginative writing**    23

# Review your skills

## Check up

Review your response to the exam-style question on page 23. Tick ✓ the column to show how well you think you have done each of the following.

| | Not quite ✓ | Nearly there ✓ | Got it! ✓ |
|---|---|---|---|
| planned a satisfying ending | ☐ | ☐ | ☐ |
| written an engaging opening | ☐ | ☐ | ☐ |
| structured your story to create impact | ☐ | ☐ | ☐ |

Look over all your work in this unit.

Note down ✐ the three most important things to remember when structuring your ideas for imaginative writing.

1. ...................................................................................................................
...................................................................................................................

2. ...................................................................................................................
...................................................................................................................

3. ...................................................................................................................
...................................................................................................................

## Need more practice?

Plan your response to the exam-style question below.

**Exam-style question**

Write a story about a time when you forgot something.

Your response could be real or imagined.

(40 marks)

How confident do you feel about each of these **skills?** Colour ✐ in the bars.

**1** How do I create a satisfying ending? ▭▭▭▭

**2** How do I engage my readers from the very beginning? ▭▭▭▭

**3** How can I structure my writing for impact? ▭▭▭▭

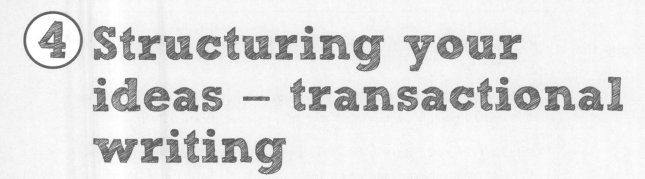

# 4 Structuring your ideas – transactional writing

This unit will help you learn how to structure your ideas in a transactional writing task. The skills you will build are to:

- sequence your ideas effectively
- plan an effective introduction
- plan an effective conclusion.

In the exam, you will be asked to tackle writing tasks such as the one below. This unit will prepare you to write your own response to this question.

---

**Exam-style question**

Write an article for a newspaper exploring the importance of money.
You could write about:

- why money is important
- whether people worry too much about money
- the ways in which money can influence people's choices and behaviour
  as well as any other ideas you might have.

(40 marks)

---

The three key questions in the **skills boosts** will help you to structure your ideas in a transactional writing task.

 **1** How do I sequence my ideas?

 **2** How do I write an effective introduction?

 **3** How do I write an effective conclusion?

Look at one student's plan to the task on the next page.

| | |
|---|---|
| Introduction | You need money to live: food, clothing, flat or house, bills, etc. But how much do you need? |
| 1 | People do terrible things for money: get into crime, fall out with friends, get into debt... it could be said that it creates more problems than it solves. |
| 2 | People do the best paid jobs they can, even if they hate the job, so that they have lots of money to spend on buying posh cars, big houses and lots of stuff. Would they be happier with less stuff and a less well-paid job that they actually enjoy? |
| 3 | We spend lots of money getting stuff that we end up throwing away. If we kept the old car, the old television and the old mobile phone, then we could save money and not be filling up the earth with waste. |
| 4 | Some people always want more. They spend their lives working, spend no time with their family and don't have the time to enjoy the things that money can buy or the things that money can't buy. |
| Conclusion | Would you rather have lots of money and be lonely? Or have a happy family life and have just enough money? Don't be greedy. Be happy. |

Look carefully at the plan above, thinking about each of the areas below. Write 🖊 a sentence or two commenting on each area, and then assess its effectiveness by awarding it a mark out of 5.

**An effective introduction:** does it introduce the topic clearly? Will it engage the reader?

....................................................................................................

....................................................................................................

....................................................................................................        /5

**An effective conclusion:** does it effectively sum up the writer's ideas? Will it have a lasting impact on the reader?

....................................................................................................

....................................................................................................

....................................................................................................        /5

**Sequencing of key points:** is the sequence of ideas logical? Could they be sequenced more logically?

....................................................................................................

....................................................................................................

....................................................................................................        /5

How do I sequence my ideas?

If you are expressing your view on a topic, you need to sequence your ideas logically, so that one idea leads to, and is developed by, the next. One way to achieve this is to think of more ideas than you will use. You can then select the ideas that are more relevant and more closely linked.

① Look at this exam-style question.

**Exam-style question**

Write the text for a speech giving your views on schools and education.

Now look at these six ideas that one student noted in a plan written in response to the exam-style question above.

1. Schools should teach you things that will help you in adult life, like cooking and how to look after your money. ☐

2. Education is important because it can help you decide which job you want and help you get that job. ☐

3. Education is important because it prepares you for adult life. ☐

4. If we did more sport at school, it would help everyone keep fit and healthy. ☐

5. Schools could do more to teach a bigger range of subjects so there is something for everyone. ☐

6. Some teachers are really unfair. They should treat all students the same. ☐

**a** Are there any points in the plan that you could be linked by turning two separate points into one more fully developed point? Underline Ⓐ these points.

**b** Now think about which **three** or **four** points you would keep and sequence. Think about:
   • which ideas are most relevant and engaging
   • which ideas are most closely linked.

Tick ✓ the three or four ideas that you would keep and sequence.

Cross ✗ the ones that you would not include in your response.

**c** In what order would you sequence the points you have ticked? Use the space below ✎ to try two or three different ideas and then underline Ⓐ your final decision.

**Unit 4 Structuring your ideas – transactional writing**    27

## ② How do I write an effective introduction?

An introduction should not simply list all the ideas that will follow in the rest of the text. An effective introduction introduces the topic, introduces your views on it, and engages the reader's interest.

① Look at the sentences below. They are all taken from different students' introductions written in response to this exam-style question.

**Exam-style question**

Write the text for a speech giving your views on schools and education.

**A.** In this article, I am going to write about schools and education.

**B.** As soon as we're old enough, everybody in this country goes to school for at least eleven years.

**C.** You cannot spend eleven or more years at school without having an opinion about it.

**D.** Love it or hate it, our school years are probably the most important years of our lives.

**E.** However, if schools do not help young people to achieve their full potential, then all the teachers' and students' time and hard work is being wasted.

**F.** I am going to consider why school and education are so important, why some people do not like school, and how it could be made more enjoyable and useful.

**G.** So how do we make sure that everybody gets what they need from their education?

ⓐ Tick ✓ the sentences that you might use to build an effective introduction to this task.

ⓑ Cross ✗ the sentences that would not effectively introduce this task.

ⓒ In what order would you sequence your chosen sentences? Write your order here.

...................................................................................................................

② Now write ✐ an introduction to the exam-style task below, aiming to:
• introduce the topic of the text  • introduce your views on the topic  • engage the reader's interest.

**Exam-style question**

Write an article for a newspaper exploring the importance of money.

...................................................................................................................
...................................................................................................................
...................................................................................................................
...................................................................................................................
...................................................................................................................
...................................................................................................................

## ③ How do I write an effective conclusion?

A conclusion should emphasise your ideas, not simply repeat them. The most effective conclusions lead the reader to think about the future by focusing on the benefits of agreeing with, or acting on, the ideas explored in the text.

① Below are the plans and conclusions, written by two different students in response to this exam-style task.

**Exam-style question**

Write an article for a newspaper exploring the importance of money.

### Student A

**Plan**
- We can't live without money: food, clothes etc.
- It's fun to go shopping and have the latest gadgets. We all do it and we all want them.
- However, there are lots of things that money cannot buy: friends, love etc.

In conclusion, money is obviously important to pay for essential things like food and clothes. It's also really nice to spend money and enjoy what you buy. However, it's not as important as your friends and family.

### Student B

**Plan**
- We spend far too much time thinking about, earning and spending money.
- People think money makes them happy because it buys them everything they want.
- Money is like a drug. You can get addicted and want more and more of it.

Not having any money can definitely make you miserable, but having loads of money doesn't always make you happy. My friends, family make me happy – and they don't cost me a penny. Perhaps we would all be happier if we spent more time thinking about other people and less time thinking about how much money we can make for ourselves.

② ⓐ Identify the following in one, or both, of the conclusions. Underline Ⓐ and label ✎ where:

   A. the writer repeats their key points

   B. the writer emphasises a key idea without repeating it

   C. the writer focuses on the benefits of agreeing with, or acting on, their ideas.

ⓑ Which conclusion would have a greater impact on readers? Tick it. ✓

ⓒ Write ✎ a sentence or two explaining your choice. ..................................................

................................................................................................................................

................................................................................................................................

................................................................................................................................

**Unit 4 Structuring your ideas – transactional writing**   **29**

# Sample response

An effectively structured transactional text should include:

- an introduction that introduces the topic and the writer's views, and engages the reader
- logically sequenced key points
- a conclusion that sums up your ideas and their benefits.

Now look at this exam-style writing task, which you saw at the start of the unit.

**Exam-style question**

Write an article for a newspaper exploring the importance of money.
You could write about:

- why money is important
- whether people worry too much about money
- the ways in which money can influence people's choices and behaviour
  as well as any other ideas you might have.

(40 marks)

Look at one student's plan in response to the task.

*Introduction:* Money is important. You can't do anything without it.

1. Imagine a world without money: you would have to grow your own food and make everything you wanted because you couldn't buy it.

2. Money makes things happen. It makes people do great things, for example inventions.

3. Having money means you don't have to worry about not having money because you can't live without it.

*Conclusion:* Sum up.

(1) What advice would you give this student to improve their plan? Note ✐ three suggestions.

a ........................................................................................................

........................................................................................................

........................................................................................................

........................................................................................................

b ........................................................................................................

........................................................................................................

........................................................................................................

........................................................................................................

c ........................................................................................................

........................................................................................................

........................................................................................................

........................................................................................................

# Your turn!

You are now going to write your response to this exam-style task.

**Exam-style question**

Write an article for a newspaper exploring the importance of money.
You could write about:

- why money is important
- whether people worry too much about money
- the ways in which money can influence people's choices and behaviour
  as well as any other ideas you might have.

(40 marks)

Use the activities below to help you identify your views and gather some ideas.

1. How important is money? Circle (A) your response on the scale below.

| 0 | 1 | 2 | 3 | 4 | 5 | 6 | 7 | 8 | 9 | 10 |

0 = not at all important; 10 = the most important thing in the world

2. Why is money important? Note 🖉 up to three reasons.

........................................................................................................

........................................................................................................

........................................................................................................

........................................................................................................

3. Why is money not important? Note 🖉 up to three reasons.

........................................................................................................

........................................................................................................

........................................................................................................

........................................................................................................

4. Write 🖉 one or two sentences summarising your views on the importance of money.

........................................................................................................

........................................................................................................

........................................................................................................

........................................................................................................

5. Now plan 🖉 your response to the above exam-style question on paper. Aim to:

   a. gather and sequence your key points

   b. write an introduction in full

   c. write a conclusion in full.

**Unit 4 Structuring your ideas – transactional writing**    31

# Review your skills

## Check up

Review your response to the exam-style question on page 31. Tick ✓ the column to show how well you think you have done each of the following.

| | Not quite ✓ | Nearly there ✓ | Got it! ✓ |
|---|---|---|---|
| sequenced my ideas | ☐ | ☐ | ☐ |
| written an effective introduction | ☐ | ☐ | ☐ |
| written an effective conclusion | ☐ | ☐ | ☐ |

Look over all of your work in this unit. Note down ✐ three things that you should remember to do when structuring a transactional text.

1. ......................................................................................................................................

2. ......................................................................................................................................

3. ......................................................................................................................................

## Need more practice?

Plan your response to the task below.

**Exam-style question**

Write the text for a speech giving your views on the importance of being an individual.

In your speech you could:

• consider ways in which people are influenced by their peers

• explore the consequences of wanting to be popular and fit in

• consider whether we should worry about how other people see us as well as any other ideas you might have.

(40 marks)

How confident do you feel about each of these **skills?** Colour ✐ in the bars.

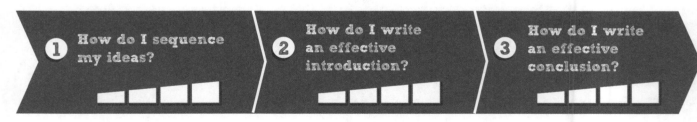

**1** How do I sequence my ideas?  ☐☐☐☐

**2** How do I write an effective introduction?  ☐☐☐☐

**3** How do I write an effective conclusion?  ☐☐☐☐

# ⑤ Cohesion – making it clear

This unit will help you learn how to give your writing cohesion: guiding the reader through your ideas by linking them clearly and fluently. The skills you will build are to:

- use adverbials as signposts to guide the reader through your writing

- use synonyms to develop ideas without repetition

- use pronouns clearly and accurately.

In the exam, you will be asked to tackle writing tasks such as the ones below. This unit will prepare you to write your own responses to these questions.

## Paper 1

**Exam-style question**

Write about a time when a wish came true.

Your response could be real or imagined.　　　　　　　　　　　　　　　　(40 marks)

## Paper 2

**Exam-style question**

Write an article for a newspaper giving your views about fame.

You could write about:

- the different ways in which people become famous

- how we treat celebrities

- why people enter and watch television talent shows such as *X Factor* and *Britain's Got Talent* as well as any other ideas you might have.　　　　　　　　　　(40 marks)

The three key questions in the **skills boosts** will help you to achieve cohesion in your writing by linking your ideas fluently and clearly.

**①** How do I guide the reader through my writing?

**②** How do I develop ideas without repeating myself?

**③** How do I link my ideas fluently and clearly?

Look at extracts from one student's answers to the tasks on the next page.

## Paper 1

**Exam-style question**

Write about a time when a wish came true.

I have only ever made one wish. My wish came true. And I will never make another wish as long as I live.

When I was nine, I hated going to school. I don't hate school anymore, but I hated school in those days. Every morning I would go to school, sit in school and wish I wasn't in school. I would wish that something would happen so that I didn't have to go to school. One day I decided I couldn't go to school anymore. That night, I wished and wished that I wouldn't have to go to school the next morning. I lay in bed wishing and wishing until I went to sleep.

The next morning I woke up with a strange pain in my stomach. I called my mum. I told her I had a strange pain in my stomach. She called the doctor. Before the school bell had gone, I was in an ambulance.

## Paper 2

**Exam-style question**

Write an article for a newspaper giving your views about fame.

People love celebrities and they all want to be one. They think they lead amazing lives all the time. They don't know what it is like. How could they know how they spend their lives when they're not in the public eye? They do not spend all their time living in mansions and going to film premiers and lying around the pool in the sunshine. They don't know what it's like to have a private life. They spend their time being followed and bothered by the newspapers trying to take their picture and they get bought in their millions because they want to see them looking like them.

(1) Which of the responses above is most clearly written? Which is most fluently written? How could they be written more clearly and fluently? Note 🖉 your advice below.

a The writer of the response to the Paper 1 writing task could ................................................................

.............................................................................................................................................................

.............................................................................................................................................................

.............................................................................................................................................................

b The writer of the response to the Paper 2 writing task could ................................................................

.............................................................................................................................................................

.............................................................................................................................................................

.............................................................................................................................................................

# How do I guide the reader through my writing?

Adverbials modify verbs: for example, he ran **quickly** but fell **suddenly**. You can also use some adverbials to link ideas and guide the reader through your writing.

**(1)** Some adverbials can signal information about time and sequencing. For example:

| Firstly | Secondly | Then | Next | Meanwhile | After several weeks | Eventually | Finally |

Look at this equation.

2 eggs + 100g self-raising flour + 100g sugar + cake tin + 180°C (× 25 minutes) = cake

Use adverbials like the ones above to rewrite the equation in full sentences, clearly explaining the sequence of events that needs to be completed in order to bake a cake.

........................................................................................................................................

........................................................................................................................................

........................................................................................................................................

**(2)** Some adverbials can guide the reader by signalling more complex relationships between ideas. They can signal:

**contradiction**, e.g.  | however | | on the other hand |

**exemplification**, e.g.  | for example | | for instance |

**cause and effect**, e.g.  | as a result | | consequently | | therefore |

**elaboration**, e.g.  | in other words | | to put it simply | | that is to say |

**emphasis**, e.g.  | above all | | indeed | | significantly |

**addition**, e.g.  | additionally | | moreover | | furthermore |

**a** Look at the sentences below. Add appropriate adverbials in the blank spaces to link them.

Every year, television talent shows attract thousands of people, looking for fame.
.................................................... very few are successful.
.................................................... most are sent home disappointed or humiliated or both.
.................................................... even the successful ones are forgotten within a year.

**b** Adverbials can be positioned at a number of different points in a sentence without affecting its meaning. Choose **one** of the sentences above. Rewrite the sentence, positioning the adverbial at a different point. ....................................................................................................

........................................................................................................................................

........................................................................................................................................

## 2 How do I develop ideas without repeating myself?

In a text, there will always be key ideas that you will need to keep referring to. Think about using **synonyms** – words or phrases with a similar meaning – to avoid repeating yourself.

> **Synonyms:** words or phrases with a similar meaning

1. Look at these two exam-style writing tasks.

**Paper 1**

**Exam-style question**

Write about a time when a wish came true.

**Paper 2**

**Exam-style question**

Write an article for a newspaper giving your views about fame.

It's very easy to end up repeating some key words in a writing task.

> **Fame** is something that many of us think we want. However, **fame** brings its own problems. For example, **fame** can mean the end of your private life.

However, this student could have replaced some of the repeated uses of the word 'fame' with:

- synonyms, e.g. | stardom | | celebrity | | popularity | | recognition |

- different forms of the key word, e.g. | being famous |

- or both, e.g. | being a star | | being a celebrity |

Rewrite ✐ the sentences above, removing all the repetition.

.................................................................................................................
.................................................................................................................
.................................................................................................................

2. Now look at these sentences, taken from one student's response to the Paper 1-style question above.

> When I was little, I thought I could make a wish and my wish would come true. When I was little, I made a wish that my mum and dad would take me to Disneyland. I wished and wished and wished every night but still it did not come true.

a. Underline Ⓐ any repeated words in the sentences above.

b. Rewrite ✐ the text, removing any repetition.

.................................................................................................................
.................................................................................................................
.................................................................................................................
.................................................................................................................
.................................................................................................................

# 3 How do I link my ideas fluently and clearly?

Referring back to ideas you have explored in previous sentences or paragraphs helps you to develop your ideas. Using carefully chosen pronouns helps the reader to follow them.

**1** Now look at some sentences from one student's response to the Paper 2-style task on page 36.

> Social media makes it easy to send famous people flattering fan mail or vicious hate mail. It can probably cause serious unhappiness or even depression.

Look carefully at the pronoun 'it' in the third sentence above. What does 'it' refer back to? Tick ✓ your choice.

**a** social media ☐    **b** flattering fan mail ☐    **c** vicious hate mail ☐

**2** Choosing carefully how you refer back to previous ideas can make your writing much easier for your reader to follow. Compare two versions of sentences from one student's response to the Paper 2-style task above.

**Version 1**

☐
> Television talent shows can create new stars very quickly. They give instant exposure to an enormous audience.
> As a result, they can become famous overnight.

**Version 2**

☐
> Television talent shows can create new stars very quickly. These programmes give instant exposure to an enormous audience. As a result, the contestants can become famous overnight.

**a** Which version is most clearly expressed? Tick it. ✓

**b** Underline Ⓐ the pronouns in Version 1 that might confuse the reader.

**c** Underline Ⓐ the words or phrases in Version 2 that have replaced them.

**3** Now look at these sentences, taken from another student's response to the Paper 1-style task above.

> My hands shook as I held the envelope and I remembered my wish from the night before. It was small and brown but it might change my life. They fumbled as I clumsily tore it open.

**a** Underline Ⓐ any pronouns that might confuse the reader.

**b** Rewrite ✏️ the sentences, expressing them as clearly and as fluently as possible.

.......................................................................................................

.......................................................................................................

.......................................................................................................

.......................................................................................................

.......................................................................................................

.......................................................................................................

.......................................................................................................

**Unit 5 Cohesion – making it clear    37**

# Sample response

To make your writing as clear and fluent as possible you should:

- use adverbials to link your ideas and guide the reader through them

- avoid repetition by varying the forms of key words or replacing them with synonyms

- use pronouns carefully, making it clear what they refer back to.

Now look at this exam-style writing task, which you saw at the start of the unit.

**Exam style question**

Write about a time when a wish came true.

Your response could be real or imagined.

(40 marks)

Look at this sample answer.

My mum bought me a hamster when I started secondary school. She bought me an amazing cage to keep the hamster in, full of runs and tunnels and secret hideaways. I called it Billy.

I loved that little hamster.

One day, I woke up and went to see the hamster. I looked in the cage. The cage was empty. I looked behind the cage. I looked all over my room. I looked all over the house. It was gone. I was so upset I didn't know what to do. That was when I made my wish. I wished that it would come home.

(1) How would you improve the fluency and clarity of this paragraph?

a Underline (A) any parts of the text that you feel could be expressed more clearly and fluently.

b Adjust the text above or rewrite (✎) it below, thinking about:

- adverbials to guide the reader
- synonyms to avoid repetition
- careful use of pronouns to refer back to previous ideas.

......................................................................................................................................................

......................................................................................................................................................

......................................................................................................................................................

......................................................................................................................................................

......................................................................................................................................................

......................................................................................................................................................

......................................................................................................................................................

......................................................................................................................................................

......................................................................................................................................................

......................................................................................................................................................

......................................................................................................................................................

# Your turn!

Choose one of the two exam-style tasks that you saw at the beginning of this unit.

## Paper 1

**Exam-style question**

Write about a time when a wish came true.

Your response could be real or imagined.                                    (40 marks)

## Paper 2

**Exam-style question**

Write an article for a newspaper giving your views about fame.

You could write about:

• the different ways in which people become famous

• how we treat celebrities

• why people enter and watch television talent shows such as *X Factor* and *Britain's Got Talent* as well as any other ideas you might have.                                    (40 marks)

You are going to **plan** and **write** the first two or three paragraphs of your response, focusing on expressing your ideas clearly and fluently.

1 Think about all the different ideas you might include in your response. Note 🖉 them in the space below.

2 a Choose the ideas that you will focus on in the opening two or three paragraphs of your response. Tick ✓ them.

b Number 🖉 your chosen ideas in the order in which you will use them.

3 Now write 🖉 the first two or three paragraphs of your response to your chosen task on paper, thinking carefully about:

• using adverbials to link your ideas and guide the reader through them

• avoiding repetition by varying the forms of key words or replacing them with synonyms

• using pronouns carefully, making it clear what they refer back to.

# Review your skills

## Check up

Look closely and carefully at your response to the exam-style question on page 39. Tick ✓ the column to show how well you think you have done each of the following.

| | Not quite ✓ | Nearly there ✓ | Got it! ✓ |
|---|---|---|---|
| guided the reader through my ideas using adverbials | ☐ | ☐ | ☐ |
| made my writing more fluent by removing some repetition | ☐ | ☐ | ☐ |
| made it clear what any pronouns I have used refer back to | ☐ | ☐ | ☐ |

Look over all your work in this unit. Note down ✐ the three most important things to remember to make your writing clear.

1. ......................................................................................................

2. ......................................................................................................

3. ......................................................................................................

## Need more practice?

You could:

- finish your response to the task you started on page 39
- tackle the other writing task on page 39.

Whichever task you tackle, remember to focus on expressing your ideas clearly and fluently.

How confident do you feel about each of these **skills?** Colour ✐ in the bars.

1. **How do I guide the reader through my writing?**
2. **How do I develop ideas without repeating myself?**
3. **How do I link my ideas fluently and clearly?**

Use sentence structures for clarity, purpose and effect (AO6)

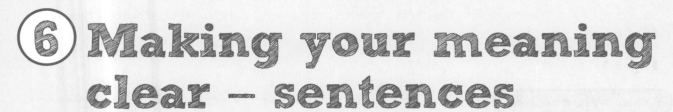

# ⑥ Making your meaning clear – sentences

This unit will help you express your ideas clearly and precisely. The skills you will build are to:

- use conjunctions to link ideas clearly
- use subject–verb sentence openings to express ideas clearly
- use punctuation accurately to express your ideas clearly.

In the exam, you will be asked to tackle writing tasks such as the ones below. This unit will prepare you to write your own response to one of these questions.

## Paper 1

**Exam-style question**

Write about a time when you, or someone you know, had to take on some responsibility.

You could write about:
- a time when you looked after a child or an adult who needed help
- a time when you had a responsible position in school, in a job or in a club.

Your response could be real or imagined.

(40 marks)

## Paper 2

**Exam-style question**

Write an article for a magazine exploring the pressures facing young people today.

In your article, you could:
- consider the issue of peer pressure from friends
- consider the pressures of education and exams
- suggest ways in which young people can cope with the pressures that they face as well as any other ideas you might have.

(40 marks)

The three key questions in the **skills boosts** will help you to make your meaning clear.

**1** How do I link my ideas to make my meaning clear?

**2** How can I structure sentences to make key ideas clear?

**3** How do I use punctuation to make my meaning clear?

Look at extracts from one student's answers to the tasks on the next page.

Look carefully at these extracts from two students' responses to the exam-style writing tasks on page 41.

## Paper 1

**Exam-style question**

Write an article for a magazine exploring the pressures facing young people today.

Teenagers live their lives under constant pressure. Many adults think that teenagers live fun and carefree lives but they could not be more wrong. Adults see teenagers standing around the high street or hanging around the park and they think we're doing nothing. Those adults do not realise what is going on beneath the surface. It looks like we're checking our phones to see what we're doing at the weekend. Actually, we're checking what people are saying about us on social media. It looks like we're having a laugh and messing about with our friends. Actually, we're trying to take our minds off the argument we had with a friend at the weekend. Above all, we're taking our minds off the fact that we should be revising for our exams if we don't want to spend the rest of our lives sleeping in a bin and living off leftovers from the bins round the back of the supermarket.

Social media is great. You can chat to friends wherever they are. It can also cause problems. Teenagers are under pressure to be on social media all the time.

## Paper 2

**Exam-style question**

Write about a time when you, or someone you know, had to take on some responsibility.

My mum left me in charge of my little brother for a whole day when I was just thirteen. It was the worst day of my life.

I wanted to watch the TV. George had other plans. While I was looking for the remote control, he quietly went to his toy cupboard. He pulled out all his cuddly toys, his building bricks, his books, his felt pens, his football, his rugby ball. He threw them on the floor, stood in the middle of them, folded his arms and stared at me. It was play time whether I liked it or not.

I told George I didn't want to play anymore. George told me he was going to start crying and tell mummy I was horrible. Then I had a really stupid idea. I decided we should make a cake. I found a recipe book and got the ingredients out of the cupboard. While I was busy turning on the oven, George dropped two eggs on the floor. I screamed. By the time I had found a cloth, George was making a cake on the kitchen floor. He had added flour and sugar to the eggs and was stirring the mixture with his feet. That was when Mum came home. She started screaming.

# How do I link my ideas to make my meaning clear?

Related ideas can be linked together in sentences. For example, look at this sentence from the responses to the writing tasks on page 42.

> Many adults think that teenagers live fun and carefree lives.

> They could not be more wrong.

These two pieces of information can be linked with the conjunction 'but' which indicates that the second piece of information contradicts the first piece of information.

> Many adults think that teenagers live fun and carefree lives | but | they could not be more wrong.

The conjunction 'but' indicates that the second piece of information contradicts the first piece of information.

**1** Look at these three pieces of information, taken from the student's response to task 1 on page 42.

> Social media is great. | You can chat to friends wherever they are. | It can also cause problems.

**a** Experiment 🖊 with **three** different ways of linking all the pieces of information into a single sentence, using conjunctions to clearly indicate how they are connected. You could choose some conjunctions from the bank on the right.

| Conjunctions bank | | | |
|---|---|---|---|
| and | but | if | because |
| when | unless | so | although |

i. ................................................................................

ii. ...............................................................................

iii. ..............................................................................

**b** Which of your three sentences above is most clearly expressed? Tick it. ✓

**c** Which of your three sentences above is least clearly expressed? Cross it. ✗

**2** **a** Write 🖊 three short sentences giving your views about the pressures that social media places on young people.

................................................................................

................................................................................

................................................................................

**b** Use the space below to experiment with linking your three sentences. You could:

- link two sentences together with a conjunction and leave one as a short sentence.
- link all three sentences together using conjunctions. 🖊

................................................................................

................................................................................

................................................................................

**c** Which of your experiments most clearly and powerfully expresses your ideas? Tick it. ✓

## 2 How can I structure sentences to make key ideas clear?

When you want to make a key point, or give the reader key information, you need to express it as clearly and powerfully as possible. One way of doing this is to use a short sentence that begins with a subject–verb construction. For example:

> Teenagers live their lives under constant pressure.

This is the verb in this short sentence. It describes what teenagers **do**.

This noun is the subject of the verb. It tells the reader **who** or **what** is doing the verb.

① Look at these sentences, taken from the student responses on page 42. **Circle** Ⓐ the subject and **underline** Ⓐ the main verb in each sentence.

**a**
> Teenagers are under pressure to be on social media all the time.

**b**
> It was the worst day of my life.

**c**
> I wanted to watch the TV.

② Look at the sentences below. These are two different versions of the opening sentence from the response to the imaginative writing task on page 42, the second task.

This version begins with the conjunction 'when' and a subordinate clause. The main clause and the main subject and verb appear half way through the sentence.

> When I was just thirteen, for a whole day my mum left me in charge of my little brother. ▢

This version begins with the subject–verb construction.

> My mum left me in charge of my little brother for a whole day when I was just thirteen. ▢

Tick ✓ the version that you feel expresses this key information most clearly and write ✐ a

sentence or two explaining your choice. ..................................................................................

........................................................................................................................................

③ The sentence below is a version of the opening sentence from the response to the transactional writing task on page 42.

> Although many adults think that teenagers live fun and carefree lives, they could not be
> more wrong because teenagers actually live their lives under constant pressure. ▢

**a** Rewrite ✐ this as three short sentences, beginning each one with a subject–verb construction.

.......................................................................................................................... ▢

.......................................................................................................................... ▢

.......................................................................................................................... ▢

**b** Tick ✓ the version that presents this information most clearly.

④ Now write ✐ three, short sentences on paper giving your ideas about the pressures facing teenagers. Begin each sentence with a subject–verb construction.

# ③ How do I use punctuation to make my meaning clear?

When you are crafting sentences, getting your punctuation in the right places is vital if you want to make your meaning clear. You **can** separate two pieces of information with a full stop or link two pieces of information with a conjunction such as 'and', 'because' or 'when'. You **cannot** link two pieces of information in a single sentence using a comma.

① **a** Which of these sentences are correctly punctuated? Mark them with a tick ✓ or a cross ✗.

i. | Social media is great. You can chat to friends wherever they are. | ☐

ii. | Social media is great, you can chat to friends wherever they are. | ☐

iii. | Social media is great because you can chat to friends wherever they are. | ☐

**b** Annotate 🖉 the sentences above, explaining why they are wrongly or correctly punctuated.

② When a sentence begins with a conjunction such as 'when' or 'if', you should use a comma to separate the subordinate clause from the main clause.

> **Remember:** A **main clause** contains the main piece of information in a sentence. A **subordinate clause** is linked to it with a subordinating conjunction such as 'when', 'because', 'if', 'although', etc.

**a** Which of these sentences are correctly punctuated? Mark them with a tick ✓ or a cross ✗.

i. | My mum left me in charge of my little brother for a whole day, I was just thirteen. | ☐

ii. | My mum left me in charge of my little brother for a whole day. I was just thirteen. | ☐

iii. | My mum left me in charge of my little brother for a whole day when I was just thirteen. | ☐

iv. | When I was just thirteen, my mum left me in charge of my little brother for a whole day. | ☐

**b** Annotate 🖉 the sentences above, explaining why they are wrongly or correctly punctuated.

Commas should be used to mark a list of items or a list of events. For example:

> *He pulled out all his cuddly toys, his building bricks, his books, his felt-tip pens, his football and his rugby ball. He threw them on the floor, stood in the middle of them, folded his arms and stared at me.*

③ Look at the text below, taken from a draft version of the response to the first task on page 42. Punctuate 🖉 it accurately. You will need to add: three full stops, three capital letters and four commas. Rewrite the text on paper.

> *when adults see teenagers standing around the high street they think we're doing nothing they don't understand the pressure we're under friends exams homework the future and even fashion are all big worries for teenagers*

# Sample response

To make your meaning clear, you need to craft carefully structured sentences, thinking about:

- using short sentences with subject–verb starts to express key ideas or information
- longer sentences using conjunctions to clearly link ideas
- accurate use of full stops and commas.

Now look at this exam-style writing task, which you saw at the start of the unit.

**Exam-style question**

Write about a time when you, or someone you know, had to take on some responsibility.

(40 marks)

You could write about:
- a time when you looked after a child or an adult who needed help
- a time when you had a responsible position in school, in a job or in a club.

Your response could be real or imagined.

Look at this extract from a draft version of the response on page 42.

> As I was beginning to lose my temper I had a really stupid idea, I decided we should make a cake. I found a recipe book and got the flour and the eggs and the butter and the sugar out of the cupboard. While I was turning on the oven George dropped two eggs on the floor while I was trying to find a cloth George decided it would be easier to make the cake on the floor and started tipping flour and sugar on top of the broken eggs and that was when Mum came home and started screaming.

How could the structure and punctuation of these sentences be improved to make the writer's meaning clearer? Redraft 🖉 them in the space below.

..............................................................................................................................
..............................................................................................................................
..............................................................................................................................
..............................................................................................................................
..............................................................................................................................
..............................................................................................................................
..............................................................................................................................
..............................................................................................................................
..............................................................................................................................
..............................................................................................................................
..............................................................................................................................
..............................................................................................................................

# Your turn!

Choose one of the two exam-style tasks that you saw at the beginning of this unit.

> ### Exam-style question
>
> Write about a time when you, or someone you know, had to take on some responsibility.
>
> **(40 marks)**
>
> You could write about:
> - a time when you looked after a child or an adult who needed help
> - a time when you had a responsible position in school, in a job or in a club.
>
> Your response could be real or imagined.

> ### Exam-style question
>
> Write an article for a magazine exploring the pressures facing young people today.
>
> In your article, you could:
> - consider the issue of peer pressure from friends
> - consider the pressures of education and exams
> - suggest ways in which young people can cope with the pressures that they face as well as any other ideas you might have.
>
> **(40 marks)**

You are going to **plan** and **write** the first two or three paragraphs of your response, focusing on sentence structure.

**1** Think about all the different ideas you might include in your response. Note them in the space below.

**2 a** Choose the ideas that you will focus on in the opening two or three paragraphs of your response. Tick them.

**b** Number your chosen ideas in the order in which you will use them.

**3** Now write the first two or three paragraphs of your response to your chosen task on paper, thinking carefully about:
- using short sentences with subject–verb starts to express key ideas or information
- using longer sentences with conjunctions clearly linking your ideas
- accurate use of full stops and commas.

# Review your skills

## Check up

Look closely and carefully at your response to the exam-style question on page 47. Tick ✓ the column to show how well you think you have done each of the following.

| | Not quite ✓ | Nearly there ✓ | Got it! ✓ |
|---|---|---|---|
| expressed key ideas clearly using short sentences with subject-verb starts | ☐ | ☐ | ☐ |
| linked ideas clearly using conjunctions in longer sentences | ☐ | ☐ | ☐ |
| improved the structure of any sentences by: a. breaking long sentences into two or more short sentences to highlight key ideas | ☐ | ☐ | ☐ |
| b. linking shorter sentences with conjunctions to form longer sentences and make my meaning clearer | ☐ | ☐ | ☐ |
| used full stops and commas accurately | ☐ | ☐ | ☐ |

Look over all your work in this unit. Note down ✎ the three most important things to remember to make your writing clear.

1. ......................................................................................................................

2. ......................................................................................................................

3. ......................................................................................................................

## Need more practice?

You could:

- finish your response to the task you started on page 47
- tackle the other writing task on page 47.

Whichever task you tackle, remember to focus on sentence structure by experimenting with different ways of structuring sentences to express your ideas as clearly as possible.

How confident do you feel about each of these **skills?** Colour ✎ in the bars.

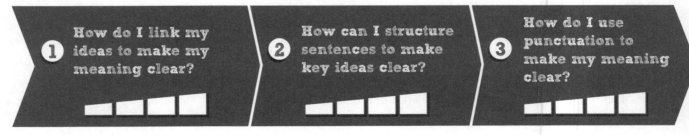

1. How do I link my ideas to make my meaning clear?

2. How can I structure sentences to make key ideas clear?

3. How do I use punctuation to make my meaning clear?

**Use a range of vocabulary and sentence structures for clarity, purpose and effect (AO6)**

# (7) Writing paragraphs and sentences to create impact

This unit will help you learn how to write paragraphs and sentences that create impact. The skills you will build are to:

- structure paragraphs and sentences for impact and effect
- select punctuation for impact and effect.

In the exam, you will be asked to tackle writing tasks such as the ones below. This unit will prepare you to write your own response to one of these questions.

## Paper 1

**Exam-style question**

Write about a time when you had the time of your life.

Your response could be real or imagined.                    (40 marks)

## Paper 2

**Exam-style question**

Write a letter to a newspaper giving your views about television.

You could write about:

- the quality of television programmes that are available
- the influence that television has on our lives
- whether people will watch less television in the future
  as well as any other ideas you might have.                (40 marks)

The three key questions in the **skills boosts** will help you to write paragraphs and sentences to create impact.

| **1** How do I structure paragraphs to create impact? | **2** How do I structure sentences to create impact? | **3** How can I use punctuation to create impact? |

Look at extracts from one student's answer to the task on page 50.

## Paper 1

**Exam-style question**

Write about a time when you had the time of your life.

> We could hear it before we saw it.
>
> Thumping music and screams echoed through the night as we approached the park. I smiled nervously as excitement flooded my stomach and made it jump and churn. We turned a corner and were blinded by a blaze of flashing coloured lights and movement. Roundabouts and waltzers whirled, huge wheels span in the air at impossible speeds, and, in the distance, tiny people in tiny cars rocketed up and down on a huge roller coaster. The night was filled with shouts and screams and laughter and the smell of popcorn and hotdogs.
>
> It was amazing.

## Paper 2

**Exam-style question**

Write a letter to a newspaper giving your views about television.

> Television is killing us.
>
> Like video games, phones and computers, watching television is something we do while sitting down (or even lying down) and we can do it for hours. Lots of teenagers I know spend every evening and most of the weekend staring at a screen. It probably adds up to about fifty or more hours a week. It's not surprising that human beings are fatter, more unfit and unhealthier than we used to be. We need to turn it off, go outside and get moving.

(1) Look closely at the structure of the paragraphs and sentences in both the responses above. Annotate (✎) any paragraph or sentence that you feel is effectively structured.

In your annotations, note:

- how the writer has structured the sentence or paragraph
- the impact on the reader.

**How do I structure paragraphs to create impact?**

You need to structure paragraphs differently depending on the purpose of your writing. However, you can also structure them to engage the reader. When you write to express your point of view, each paragraph should focus on a specific topic. This topic should be clearly stated in the first, or **topic sentence** of the paragraph. The rest of the paragraph builds on this key point with evidence or examples and further detail or explanation.

1) Look at this paragraph in which the writer expresses their views about television.

> The quantity of television you could watch is amazing. Hundreds of channels broadcast thousands of hours of television every day. However, the quality of these hours of television is not as amazing as the quantity. The problem is how to find the television gems buried in all the rubbish. The solution is not to bother. Switch it off instead.

a i Label the first sentence A, the second sentence B, and so on.

ii Use the space around the paragraph to summarise the role of each sentence e.g. sentence A introduces the paragraph.

A paragraph can consist of just one short sentence. Very short paragraphs can give additional emphasis to a key point in a transactional text.

b Which sentence or sentences could you separate from the rest of the paragraph and position in their own very short paragraph to add emphasis? Separate your chosen sentence(s) from the rest of the paragraph with a double slash (//).

2) In a narrative text, you can structure a paragraph to build up to a moment of tension or drama.

- The roller coaster cars began to climb.
- I closed my eyes and listened to the blood pounding in my ears.
- My pulse was racing as the people below got smaller and smaller.
- We climbed higher and higher.
- Higher and still higher we climbed.
- We slowed down and I knew we had nearly reached the top.
- And then everything disappeared and we soared down into the darkness.
- I screamed and screamed until it stopped.

a Which of the sentences above would you include in a paragraph describing a ride on a roller coaster? Tick them using the boxes at the end of each sentence.

b Number your chosen sentences to show the order in which you would structure them.

c Circle any sentences that you could structure into their own very short paragraph to add dramatic emphasis.

**2** **How do I structure sentences to create impact?**

How you choose to structure your sentences can alter their impact on the reader.

① Look at the sentence below, in which a student describes a visit to a theme park.

**Version 1**

> Thumping music and screams echoed through the night as we approached the park.

Look at the different elements that the writer has linked and sequenced to build the sentence.

| Thumping music | screams | echoed | through the night | we approached the park |

There are lots of ways in which these elements could be linked and sequenced. They could be resequenced and restructured as two separate sentences, for example:

**Version 2**

> We approached the park. Through the night, screams and thumping music echoed.

**a** Experiment ✏️ with restructuring the sentence in a third way.

.............................................................................................................................

.............................................................................................................................

**b** Which version would have a greater impact on the reader – Version 1, Version 2 or your version? Write ✏️ a sentence or two explaining your choice.

.............................................................................................................................

.............................................................................................................................

.............................................................................................................................

② Now look at this sentence, in which a student expresses their views about television.

> In the future, we will get all our information and entertainment from the internet and televisions will become extinct like the dinosaurs.

**a** Restructure and/or resequence ✏️ the elements in the sentence above in two different ways.

1. ......................................................................................................................... ☐

.............................................................................................................................

2. ......................................................................................................................... ☐

.............................................................................................................................

**b** Which version would have a greater impact on the reader? Tick it. ✓

**c** Write ✏️ a sentence or two explaining your choice.

.............................................................................................................................

.............................................................................................................................

.............................................................................................................................

## ③ How can I use punctuation to create impact?

Punctuation helps to make meaning clear. Also, used carefully and sparingly, punctuation can add impact to ideas.

① Look at the sentence below, in which a student expresses their views about television.

> *Television, whether we like it or not, is a major part of our lives. And it's here to stay.*

Adding punctuation to this sentence can change its tone and emphasis. Compare these different versions of the same sentence:

**Version 1**

> *Television – whether we like it or not – is a major part of our lives... and it's here to stay.*

**Version 2**

> *Television, whether we like it or not, is a major part of our lives – and it's here to stay!*

**a** Spot the differences: circle Ⓐ all the punctuation that has been added in Version 1 and 2.

**b** Which version do you prefer: the original, Version 1 or Version 2? Write 🖉 a sentence or two explaining your choice.

.........................................................................................................................

.........................................................................................................................

.........................................................................................................................

**c** What job does each punctuation mark do? Complete 🖉 the sentences below.

| ! | The exclamation mark can be used to ........................................................... |
| — | The dash can be used to ........................................................................... |
| ⋯ | Ellipses can be used to ............................................................................ |

② Look at the sentences below in which a student describes a visit to a theme park.

> *Nothing, absolutely nothing, could have prepared me for that ride. I was terrified.*

**a** Write 🖉 two different versions of the sentences, experimenting with a range of punctuation.

A. ..................................................................................................................... ☐

.........................................................................................................................

B. ..................................................................................................................... ☐

.........................................................................................................................

**b** Which version do you prefer? Tick it ✓ and write 🖉 a sentence or two explaining your choice.

.........................................................................................................................

.........................................................................................................................

.........................................................................................................................

# Sample response

To craft paragraphs and sentences that create impact you need to think about:

- paragraph structure and length
- how you structure and sequence the different elements in your sentences
- using punctuation carefully and sparingly to add impact to your ideas.

Now look at this exam-style writing task, which you saw at the start of the unit.

**Exam-style question**

Write a letter to a newspaper giving your views about television.

You could write about:

- the quality of television programmes that are available
- the influence that television has on our lives
- whether people will watch less television in the future
  as well as any other ideas you might have.

(40 marks)

Here is a paragraph from a student's answer.

Some people think that television can have a big influence on our lives because they say that if we see crime or violence in television programmes then we will copy it. For example some children's programmes have been banned or edited to remove violence yet even very young children can tell the difference between fiction and reality and adults certainly can. Television should show the world as it really is and that means showing crime and violence. You can easily turn the television off if you don't want to see what is being shown.

(1) How would you improve this paragraph?

a Think about paragraph structure. Mark ⟨✏⟩ the text with a double slash ⟨//⟩ where you think it would add impact to start a new paragraph.

b Now think about the structure and sequence of the elements in **one or two** sentences. Use the space below to experiment with restructuring and/or re-sequencing them to add more impact. ⟨✏⟩

c Look again at the sentences that you have restructured. Could you add further impact by adding further punctuation? ⟨✏⟩

# Your turn!

You are now going to write your response to one of these exam-style tasks.

## Paper 1

**Exam-style question**

Write about a time when you had the time of your life.

Your response could be real or imagined.

(40 marks)

## Paper 2

**Exam-style question**

Write a letter to a newspaper giving your views about television.

You could write about:

- the quality of television programmes that are available

- the influence that television has on our lives

- whether people will watch less television in the future
  as well as any other ideas you might have.

(40 marks)

(1) Think about all the different ideas you might include in your response. Note ✏ them in the space below.

(2) Number ✏ your ideas in the order in which you will use them.

(3) Now write ✏ your response to your chosen task on paper, thinking carefully about:

- paragraph structure and length
- how you structure and sequence the different elements in your sentences
- using punctuation carefully and sparingly to add impact to your ideas.

# Review your skills

## Check up

Look closely and carefully at your response to the exam-style question on page 55. Tick ✓ the column to show how well you think you have done each of the following.

| | Not quite ✓ | Nearly there ✓ | Got it! ✓ |
|---|---|---|---|
| used paragraph structure to create some impact | ☐ | ☐ | ☐ |
| used sentence structure to create some impact | ☐ | ☐ | ☐ |
| used punctuation to create some impact | ☐ | ☐ | ☐ |

Look over all your work in this unit. Note down ✐ the three most important things to remember to write paragraphs and sentences to create impact.

1. ........................................................................................................

........................................................................................................

2. ........................................................................................................

........................................................................................................

3. ........................................................................................................

........................................................................................................

## Need more practice?

Tackle the other writing task on page 55.

Remember to focus on creating impact through your choice of paragraph and sentence structure, and punctuation.

How confident do you feel about each of these **skills?** Colour ✐ in the bars.

**1** How do I structure paragraphs to create impact?

**2** How do I structure sentences to create impact?

**3** How can I use punctuation to create impact?

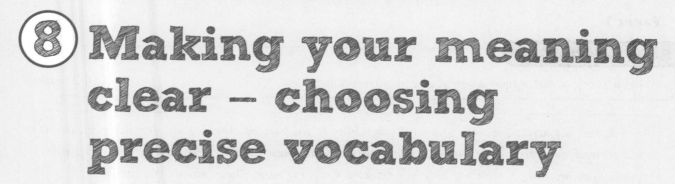

# ⑧ Making your meaning clear – choosing precise vocabulary

This unit will help you learn how to select vocabulary to help you make your meaning clear. The skills you will build are to:

- select vocabulary that helps you to achieve an appropriate register

- select vocabulary with precision

- use modification effectively to clarify your meaning.

In the exam, you will be asked to tackle writing tasks such as the ones below. This unit will prepare you to write your own response to one of these questions.

## Paper 1

**Exam-style question**

Write about a time when you were given some help.

Your response could be real or imagined.                                    (40 marks)

## Paper 2

**Exam-style question**

Write an article for a magazine giving your views about food.

You could:

- consider what we should and should not eat

- suggest ways in which people could eat more healthily

- explore how we could be made more aware of what we eat
  as well as any other ideas you might have.                                (40 marks)

The three key questions in the **skills boosts** will help you to make your meaning clear by choosing precise vocabulary.

**1** How do I choose the right words?     **2** How do I choose the best words?     **3** How do I choose vocabulary for clarity and concision?

Look at the extracts from students' answers to the tasks, on the next page.

### Paper 1

**Exam-style question**

Write a story about a time when you were given some help. **(40 marks)**

> I looked out across the dark green hills, reaching to the horizon. The sky was crowded with clouds and turning dark grey. A cold wind was beginning to blow and the bare trees swayed. Freezing rain splashed on my face, soaked my hair and trickled down my neck. There was no one in sight.
>
> A feeling of emptiness filled my stomach and a shudder crawled up my spine as I realised I had no idea where I was, how to get back to the hostel, or where everybody else was.
>
> I was lost.
>
> I wanted to sit on the ground and cry. I wanted to run up and down and over the hills to see if I could see someone or something or anything I recognised. I wanted to shout for help. I wanted to know what I should do. But I didn't. I had no idea what to do. So I sat on the ground and began to cry.

### Paper 2

**Exam-style question**

'Most of us eat far too much junk food. We should be more careful about what we eat.'

Write an article for a magazine explaining your views on this statement. **(40 marks)**

> Fast food is really bad. A big burger, fries and a drink is full of the things that are bad for us, like loads of fat, salt and sugar. They are quick and easy and quite cheap and they taste good, but they're not good for us. Even things that you think are better choices like wraps or salads or subs have loads of salt and sugar in them. You don't really know what you're eating so it's difficult to make the right choice.
>
> The best thing to do is not to eat junk food or, if you do eat it, don't eat it very often. Instead of eating junk food, you could make something really nice and healthy at home like some pasta salad or a healthy sandwich so you know what is in it and what you're eating. It might take a bit more effort and a bit more time but it will be much nicer and much better for you.

(1) Look closely at the vocabulary choices in the two extracts above.

a Underline (A) any vocabulary choices that you think are particularly effective.

b Circle (Ⓐ) any vocabulary choices that you feel could be improved. It might be that:

  • they are too formal or informal

  • they do not make the writer's meaning or ideas very clear.

c Annotate (✐) each of the vocabulary choices that you have circled, noting:

  • **why** you think they need to be improved

  • **how** you think they could be improved, e.g. some possible alternative vocabulary choices.

**How do I choose the right words?**

In almost every writing task that you are likely to tackle in an exam, it will be appropriate to write using a more formal register.

(1) Look at this exam-style question.

**Exam-style question**

Write an article for a magazine giving your views about food.

Now look at these three versions of sentences written in response to it.

**Version 1** ☐

We do not need to be reminded constantly that fast food is an unhealthy option. If we are old enough to pay for our own burger, we are old enough to make up our own minds.

**Version 2** ☐

Incessant accentuation of the negative consequences of burger consumption is unnecessary. We are perfectly capable of reaching this conclusion without additional assistance.

**Version 3** ☐

I reckon people need to stop going on about how burgers are well bad for you. We ain't kids.

**a** Which version is written in the register most appropriate to the task? Tick it. ✓

**b** Write ✐ a sentence or two explaining your choice.

.....................................................................................................................................

.....................................................................................................................................

.....................................................................................................................................

(2) Look at this exam-style question.

**Exam-style question**

Write about a time when you were given some help.

The sentences below are taken from a student's response to it. Rewrite ✐ the sentences using a more appropriate register.

He was eyeballing me and I was thinking like what you looking at? He goes, 'Need some help, mate?' and I goes, 'Maybe, yeah.'

.....................................................................................................................................

.....................................................................................................................................

.....................................................................................................................................

**Unit 8 Making your meaning clear – choosing precise vocabulary**    **59**

## ② How do I choose the best words?

Some words have more than one meaning. Using them can make your writing unclear. However, most words have a number of synonyms – that is, other words which share a similar meaning. Using a synonym with a more precise meaning can help you to express your ideas more clearly.

① Look at the sentence below, written by a student explaining their views about food.

> *The trouble is that most food that is good for you is actually really <u>bad</u>.*

Which of the meanings of 'bad' do you think the writer intends?

| | |
|---|---|
| ☐ evil<br>wicked<br>malicious | ☐ unhealthy<br>innutritious<br>harmful |
| ☐ rotten<br>decaying<br>mouldy | ☐ awful<br>unpleasant<br>appalling |
| ☐ tasteless<br>flavourless<br>bland | ☐ boring<br>unexciting<br>monotonous |
| ☐ | |

Tick ✓ the word (or two words) that you think the writer **should** have chosen to express their opinion more clearly – or you could add ✐ and tick ✓ some synonyms of your own.

② Choose a food that you strongly like or dislike.

**a** Write ✐ a sentence or two expressing your opinion of your chosen food, using at least **three** words that you have specifically selected to express your opinion **precisely**.

.......................................................................................................................................

.......................................................................................................................................

**b** Underline Ⓐ the **three** words that you have specifically selected to express your opinion. For each one, note down ✐ **at least two** synonyms.

1. ..............................................................................................................................

2. ..............................................................................................................................

3. ..............................................................................................................................

**c** Review your sentences. Do any of the synonyms that you have noted express your opinion more precisely? Tick ✓ your final choices.

③ Look at the sentence below, taken from a student's story about a time when they were given some help.

> *I fell and hit my head on the pavement. It was painful.*

Rewrite ✐ the sentence, aiming to make the description as precise and vivid as possible.

.......................................................................................................................................

.......................................................................................................................................

.......................................................................................................................................

# ③ How do I choose vocabulary for clarity and concision?

Modifying your noun and verb choices with adjectives and adverbs can make your meaning clearer and more precise. However, choosing more precise **nouns** and **verbs** can make your writing clearer, more precise **and** more concise.

① Compare these two descriptions:
- one uses mainly nouns and verbs
- the other also uses lots of adjectives and adverbials.

A.
> There was a huge, bright, blinding lightning flash and suddenly heavy rain fell from the sky.
> Soon I was extremely wet.

B.
> Lightning crackled, rain poured and I was soaked.

**a** Tick ✓ the description that you think is:

|  | A | B | Neither |
|---|---|---|---|
| • more vivid | ☐ | ☐ | ☐ |
| • more precise | ☐ | ☐ | ☐ |
| • more concise | ☐ | ☐ | ☐ |

**b** Write ✏ a sentence or two explaining your choices.

........................................................................................................

........................................................................................................

........................................................................................................

........................................................................................................

② Look at one student's views about food.

> Crisp, green lettuce, juicy, red, ripe tomatoes and succulent mouth-watering cucumber taste really lovely and nice in a great, big, fresh, healthy salad.

Rewrite ✏ the sentence above to make it more concise. By how many words can you reduce it without losing any precision of meaning?

........................................................................................................

........................................................................................................

........................................................................................................

........................................................................................................

**Unit 8 Making your meaning clear – choosing precise vocabulary**     **61**

# Sample response

When you select vocabulary for your writing you need to think about:

- writing in an appropriate register
- selecting nouns, verbs and modification that express your ideas precisely, clearly and concisely.

Now look at this exam-style writing task, which you saw at the start of the unit.

**Exam-style question**

Write an article for a magazine giving your views about food.

You could:

- consider what we should and should not eat
- suggest ways in which people could eat more healthily
- explore how we could be made more aware of what we eat
  as well as any other ideas you might have.

(40 marks)

Now look at extracts from two students' responses to it.

**Student A**

It is OK if you eat healthy food often and unhealthy food not very often. It's OK to eat unhealthy food sometimes but not all the time because it makes you unhealthy when you're older.

**Student B**

There are many seriously and greatly worrying problems with junk food. It is absolutely packed with tons of salt, gallons of fat, and piles of sugar which are extremely bad for children, adults and especially for elderly people.

(1) How effective are these students' vocabulary choices in the two extracts above?

- **a** Circle Ⓐ any inappropriately informal vocabulary choices.
- **b** Underline Ⓐ any words or phrases that could be made more precise.
- **c** Rewrite ✏ both extracts below, aiming to make vocabulary choices that are more appropriate, precise and concise.

Student A. ........................................................................................................................

..............................................................................................................................................

..............................................................................................................................................

..............................................................................................................................................

..............................................................................................................................................

Student B. ........................................................................................................................

..............................................................................................................................................

..............................................................................................................................................

..............................................................................................................................................

..............................................................................................................................................

..............................................................................................................................................

# Your turn!

You are now going to write your response to one of these exam-style tasks.

## Paper 1

**Exam-style question**

Write about a time when you were given some help.

Your response could be real or imagined.                                    (40 marks)

## Paper 2

**Exam-style question**

Write an article for a magazine giving your views about food.

You could:

- consider what we should and should not eat
- suggest ways in which people could eat more healthily
- explore how we could be made more aware of what we eat
  as well as any other ideas you might have.                               (40 marks)

(1) Think about all the different ideas you might include in your response. Note ✐ them in the space below.

(2) Number ✐ your ideas in the order in which you will use them.

(3) Now write ✐ your response to your chosen task on paper, thinking carefully about:

- using an appropriate register
- selecting nouns, verbs and modification that express your ideas precisely, clearly and concisely.

# Review your skills

## Check up

Look closely and carefully at your response to the exam-style question on page 63. Tick ✓ the column to show how well you think you have done each of the following.

| | Not quite ✓ | Nearly there ✓ | Got it! ✓ |
|---|---|---|---|
| made vocabulary choices to suit the task | ☐ | ☐ | ☐ |
| selected vocabulary that is clear and precise | ☐ | ☐ | ☐ |
| used modification to clarify meaning | ☐ | ☐ | ☐ |

Look over all your work in this unit. Note down ✏ the three most important things to remember when choosing precise vocabulary.

1. ....................................................................................................
....................................................................................................

2. ....................................................................................................
....................................................................................................

3. ....................................................................................................

## Need more practice?

Tackle the other writing task on page 63.

Remember to focus on:

• achieving an appropriate register

• selecting vocabulary to express your ideas clearly, precisely and concisely.

How confident do you feel about each of these **skills?** Colour ✏ in the bars.

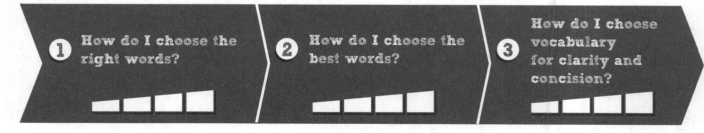

**①** How do I choose the right words?

**②** How do I choose the best words?

**③** How do I choose vocabulary for clarity and concision?

# ⑨ Selecting vocabulary for impact and effect

This unit will help you learn how to select vocabulary for impact and effect. The skills you will build are to:

- use vocabulary choices to support the intention of your writing
- use vocabulary choices to add emphasis to your ideas
- use vocabulary choices to manipulate the reader's response to your writing.

In the exam, you will be asked to tackle writing tasks such as the ones below. This unit will prepare you to write your own response to one of these questions.

## Paper 1

**Exam-style question**

Write about time when you, or someone you know, got something wrong.

Your response could be real or imagined.

(40 marks)

## Paper 2

**Exam-style question**

Write an article for a newspaper giving your views about the internet.

You could:

- consider the benefits of the internet and how it can help people
- explore the problems the internet can cause and how it can hurt people
- how the internet may develop and change our lives in the future as well as any other ideas you might have.

(40 marks)

The three key questions in the **skills boosts** will help you to select vocabulary for impact and effect.

**①** How can I use vocabulary choice to add impact to my writing?

**②** How can I choose vocabulary to help me to achieve my intention?

**③** How can I review and improve my vocabulary choices?

Look at the extracts from students' answers to the tasks on the next page.

## Paper 1

Tramping breathlessly through dense clouds of insects and the dark mud of the forest, I was beginning to think I would never find my way home, let alone find my friend's house.

Then, in a little clearing in the distance, I saw a house. My pulse began to race as I hurried to my friend's house. Relief surged through my body and I smiled happily to myself.

As I stumbled through the weeds and brambles, a crumbling old ruin loomed before me. The windows were discoloured with filth, the walls crumbling and weeds sprouting from the cracks in the bricks. Could this really be my friend's house?

I knocked quietly on the dark, wooden front door and waited. There was something in the dark shadows of that place that made me nervous. I began to back away.

And that was when I saw her at a window, lurking behind a curtain, an old woman smirking at me.

/5

## Paper 2

One way in which the internet can be bad is when people bully each other on social media. Sometimes people make comments about a person which can be quite upsetting. Those people might never say those things if they were face to face with that person. Using the internet makes people braver and more unkind because you can say anything you like about anyone and it seems like no one does anything about it. It also means that, on some social media, anybody in the world can read those nasty comments so it makes you feel like you have been humiliated in front of all your friends and in front of the whole world.

/5

① Look closely at both extracts. Which do you think has the most effective vocabulary choices? Give each one a mark out of 5, using the scale below. ✏️

| 1 | Vocabulary choices do not make the writer's meaning clear. |
|---|---|
| 2 | Vocabulary helps the writer make some of their meaning clear. |
| 3 | Vocabulary choices make the writer's meaning perfectly clear. |
| 4 | Some vocabulary choices have an impact on the reader. |
| 5 | A significant number of vocabulary choices have an impact on the reader. |

② Write ✏️ a sentence or two explaining your decisions, using examples from the two responses.

a I awarded the Paper 1 response a mark of ..................... because ......................................................

......................................................................................................................................................

......................................................................................................................................................

b I awarded the Paper 2 response a mark of ..................... because ......................................................

......................................................................................................................................................

......................................................................................................................................................

## 1 How can I use vocabulary choice to add impact to my writing?

One way to add impact to your writing is by using emotive language – that is, vocabulary choices that create a powerful emotional response in the reader.

① Look at the sentence below in which the writer expresses their views on the internet.

> Unkind comments on social media can _____ people's self esteem.

Now look at some of the verbs that could be used to fill the gap:

☐ harm    ☐ shatter    ☐ destroy    ☐ annihilate    ☐ damage    ☐ crush    ☐ affect

**a** Add 🖉 them to the table below, ranking them in order of emotiveness.

Least emotive

☐
☐
☐
☐
☐
☐

Most emotive

**b** Which verb would you choose to fill the gap in the sentence above to create the greatest impact on the reader? Tick it ✓ and write it in the sentence above.

② Now look at some of the vocabulary choices that one student considered when describing their reaction to getting something wrong.

I
- stared ☐
- gazed ☐
- looked ☐
- glared ☐

- in horror ☐
- in shock ☐
- in surprise ☐

when I realised my

- error. ☐
- mistake. ☐
- blunder. ☐

My face

- went pink ☐
- went red ☐
- burned ☐
- glowed ☐

with

- embarrassment ☐
- humiliation. ☐
- shame. ☐

**a** Which vocabulary would you choose to create the greatest impact on the reader? Tick ✓ your choices.

**b** Write 🖉 a sentence or two in which you describe yourself experiencing anger.

......................................................................................................

......................................................................................................

......................................................................................................

......................................................................................................

**c** Circle Ⓐ any vocabulary in your sentence(s) that you think would have an impact on the reader.

**Unit 9 Selecting vocabulary for impact and effect**    67

## 2 How can I choose vocabulary to help me to achieve my intention?

When you write a text, you should be aware of your **intention** – that is, the impact you intend your writing to have on the reader. Your vocabulary choices can make a significant contribution to achieving it.

When you write to present a point of view about the internet, for example, you might intend to present:

| A. a balanced point of view | i. The internet bombards us with unnecessary and unreliable information. |
| B. a negative point of view | ii. The internet contains a range of information. |
| C. a positive point of view | iii. The internet allows us to access a wealth of useful and valuable information. |

(1) (a) Draw ✏ a line linking the sentences to the point of view that they present.

(b) Circle Ⓐ the vocabulary choices in the sentences that support that point of view.

(2) Compare the writer's intention in these descriptions of **place** and **character**, taken from an imaginative writing task.

A | *As I wandered through the grass and wildflowers, a ramshackle cottage appeared in front of me.* | *Looking out of a window, an elderly lady was smiling at me.*

B | *As I stumbled through the weeds and brambles, a crumbling old ruin loomed before me.* | *Lurking behind a curtain, an old woman was smirking at me.*

(a) What impressions of place and character does each pair of sentences create?
Write ✏ a sentence summarising your ideas.

......................................................................................................................

......................................................................................................................

(b) Circle Ⓐ the words that contribute to your impression of character and place in each one.

(3) You are going to write a sentence or two describing a teenager standing on a street.

1. First, decide your intention. How will you present the teenager and the street?
Write ✏ a sentence summarising your intention.

......................................................................................................................

......................................................................................................................

2. Now write ✏ your sentences, selecting vocabulary that will help you to achieve that intention.

......................................................................................................................

......................................................................................................................

......................................................................................................................

......................................................................................................................

3. Circle Ⓐ all your vocabulary choices that contributed to achieving your intention.

## ③ How can I review and improve my vocabulary choices?

When you have finished writing, you should review your vocabulary choices to see if you can give them greater impact.

① Look at these sentences, taken from a student's response to an imaginative writing question about a time when they got something wrong.

> *I should not have said what I said. I had made a big mistake and I was really upset.*

**a** Which vocabulary choices could be replaced to give them greater impact? Circle Ⓐ them.

**b** For each word you have circled, note down 🖊 **two or three** alternative words or phrases that you could use to replace them.

Now think about how you could develop the ideas in the sentences. Which of these details could you add to give them greater impact? Note 🖊 some ideas for each one in the table.

| | |
|---|---|
| The narrator's thoughts: | |
| The narrator's physical feelings: | |
| The narrator's emotional feelings: | |

**c** Rewrite 🖊 the sentences above, using your chosen details and careful vocabulary choices to give them as much impact as possible.

........................................................................................................

........................................................................................................

........................................................................................................

........................................................................................................

② Now look at this sentence, in which a student expresses their views about the internet.

> *The internet is a good way to find information and do research.*

Rewrite 🖊 the sentence, giving it greater impact. Think about:

- how you could develop the view that the writer is expressing
- any further ideas or details you could use to develop the sentence
- vocabulary choices to give it greater impact.

........................................................................................................

........................................................................................................

........................................................................................................

........................................................................................................

# Sample response

When you select vocabulary for impact and effect, you should think about:

- using emotive language
- vocabulary that helps you to achieve your intention
- reviewing and improving your writing to make sure that you have created maximum impact with your choice of details and vocabulary.

Now look at this exam-style writing task, which you saw at the start of the unit.

**Exam-style question**

Write an article for a newspaper giving your views about the internet.

You could:

- consider the benefits of the internet and how it can help people
- explore the problems the internet can cause and how it can hurt people
- how the internet may develop and change our lives in the future
  as well as any other ideas you might have.

(40 marks)

(1) Read an extract from one student's response to the task.

> One good thing about the internet is how it can help people connect with each other. Families who have relatives in different parts of the country or in other countries can share photos and news really easily. A few years ago, people had to write letters and send photos in the post so now it is much easier. The internet has changed this a lot. The internet can make families feel not so far apart from each other.

a  What is the writer's intention in this paragraph? Write ✏ a sentence or two explaining your ideas.

.................................................................................................................................

.................................................................................................................................

.................................................................................................................................

b  Circle Ⓐ five vocabulary choices in the extract that you feel could be improved to help the writer achieve their intention or emphasise their ideas.

c  For each word or phrase you have circled, note ✏ two or three possible alternative choices, and then tick ✓ the one that you think is most effective.

.................................................................................................................................

.................................................................................................................................

.................................................................................................................................

.................................................................................................................................

# Your turn!

You are now going to write your response to one of these exam-style tasks.

## Paper 1

**Exam-style question**

Write about time when you, or someone you know, got something wrong.

Your response could be real or imagined. **(40 marks)**

## Paper 2

**Exam-style question**

Write an article for a newspaper giving your views about the internet.

You could:

- consider the benefits of the internet and how it can help people
- explore the problems the internet can cause and how it can hurt people
- how the internet may develop and change our lives in the future
  as well as any other ideas you might have. **(40 marks)**

(1) Think about all the different ideas you might include in your response. Note ✎ them in the space below.

(2) Number ✎ your ideas in the order in which you will use them.

(3) Now write ✎ your response to your chosen task on paper, thinking carefully about selecting, reviewing and improving vocabulary choices to help you to achieve your intention.

# Review your skills

## Check up

Look closely and carefully at your response to the exam-style question on page 71. Tick ✓ the column to show how well you think you have done each of the following.

|  | Not quite ✓ | Nearly there ✓ | Got it! ✓ |
|---|---|---|---|
| used emotive vocabulary choices to emphasise ideas | ☐ | ☐ | ☐ |
| selected vocabulary that helps you to achieve your intention | ☐ | ☐ | ☐ |
| reviewed and improved any vocabulary choices | ☐ | ☐ | ☐ |

Look over all your work in this unit. Note down 🖉 the three most important things to remember when selecting vocabulary for impact and effect.

1. ......................................................................................................................

2. ......................................................................................................................

3. ......................................................................................................................

## Need more practice?

Tackle the other writing task on page 71.

Remember to focus closely on selecting, reviewing and improving vocabulary choices to help you to achieve your intention.

How confident do you feel about each of these **skills?** Colour 🖉 in the bars.

**1** How can I use vocabulary choice to add impact to my writing?

**2** How can I choose vocabulary to help me to achieve my intention?

**3** How can I review and improve my vocabulary choices?

# Answers

## Unit 1

### Page 2

(1) For example: mysterious atmosphere in the opening; suspense as the narrator hears a noise; tension as the narrator goes downstairs.

### Page 5

(1) **a** The narrator of the story is the most likely hero figure. Consider ways in which she could be more in control of the situation, e.g. in the ways in which she deals with her friend and boyfriend.

**b** The most likely villain is the friend whose suggestion in the climax could be amplified to suggest some ulterior motive.

(2) For example, the reason for the boyfriend's message.

(3) For example, tension as the narrator approaches her boyfriend's house.

(4) **a** For example, adding a final twist that the narrator and her boyfriend split up a couple of days later.

**c** For example, making the party a celebration before her boyfriend emigrates!

## Unit 2

### Page 10

(2) For example, it is very important to be fit and healthy. Anyone can do it and enjoy it.

### Page 11

(1) For example, exercise, smoking, alcohol, life expectancy, illness.

### Page 13

(1) For example, 1A, 2D, 3C.

### Page 14

**Examples**

Benefits: We can live our lives and live longer.

Problems: Some people become obsessed with going to the gym; exercise isn't always good for you.

Solutions: Get the balance right.

## Unit 3

### Page 19

(1) For example, a spoilt, selfish child becomes a kind and helpful child; a distant parent becomes loving and affectionate.

(2) Endings which involve luck or a surprise (sometimes called 'deus ex machina') can be unsatisfying. Endings which have their origins embedded in the main events of the story are often far more satisfying.

(3) For example, events reveal that the invention, although useless as a water-powered car, has another unsuspected use which will make the hero wealthy or, at least, happier.

### Page 20

(1) Introducing the main character is, perhaps, the weakest opening. Each of the other three is instantly dramatic and engaging. It could be argued, however, that jumping straight into the action does not allow a build-up of tension.

### Page 21

(1) Note that, non-chronological structures are only one way to create a story with impact. They can be effective, but are not necessarily more effective than chronological structures.

In this example, it could be argued that beginning with:
* the resolution would reveal too much information
* the conflict would create instant drama and tension
* the climax might prompt questions but be less dramatic/tense.

## Unit 4

### Page 27

(4) **a** Points 2 and 3 could be linked to form a single, more developed point.

**b** Points 4 and 6 are, perhaps, the least relevant to the others.

**c** 2+3 > 1 > 5 follows a logical sequence: first considering the importance of school as a preparation for adult life, then how it could be made more relevant to adult life and, finally, how it could be made more relevant to students.

### Page 28

(1) Sentences 1 and 6 are ineffective in introducing the topic; they simply and pointlessly reiterate the task and the points that will follow. Some or all of sentences 2, 3, 4, 5 and 7 could be used to create an effective introduction, e.g. 2>4> 5.

### Page 29

(2) **a** A: All of Student A's conclusion consists of a repetition of their key points.

**b** B: 'Not having any money can definitely make you miserable, but having loads of money doesn't always make you happy.' emphasises the second point in Student B's plan.

**c** C: 'Perhaps we would all be happier if we spent more time thinking about other people and less time thinking about how much money we can make for ourselves.' emphasises the benefits of agreeing with Student B's ideas.

## Page 30

(a) All of the key points in the plan are valid. However, they could be more closely related.

(b) It could be argued that the second point is stronger than the third and they could therefore swap position to create a stronger argument.

(c) The conclusion needs to be planned to emphasise key ideas and highlight the benefits of agreeing with the reader.

# Unit 5

## Page 34

(1) (a) The writer's fluency is significantly hampered by repetition.

(b) The writer's use of pronouns – in particular, 'they' referring to both 'celebrities' and the 'people' who 'want to be one'. This reduces the text's clarity significantly.

## Page 35

(1) Firstly, mix 2 eggs, 100g self-raising flour and 100g sugar. Then place the mixture in a cake tin. Finally, place the cake tin in the oven at 180 °C for 25 minutes.

(2) (a) Every year, television talent shows attract thousands of people, looking for fame.

**However** very few are successful.

**Consequently** most are sent home disappointed or humiliated or both.

**Indeed**, even the successful ones are forgotten within a year.

(b) Very few, **however**, are successful, **or** very few are successful, **however**.

## Page 36

(1) Fame is something that many of us think we want. However, <u>being famous</u> brings its own problems. For example, <u>stardom</u> can mean the end of your private life.

(2) (a) When I was <u>little</u>, I thought I could make a <u>wish</u> and my <u>wish</u> would <u>come true</u>. When I was <u>little</u>, I <u>wished</u> that my mum and dad would take me to Disneyland. I <u>wished</u> and <u>wished</u> and <u>wished</u> every night but still it did not <u>come true</u>.

(b) When I was <u>little</u>, I thought I could make a <u>wish</u> and my <u>prayers</u> would <u>be answered</u>. When I was <u>seven</u>, I <u>prayed</u> that my mum and dad would take me to Disneyland. I <u>wished</u> and <u>prayed</u> and <u>begged</u> every night but still it did not come true.

## Page 37

(1) (c) However, readers are likely to have to work this out through contextual deduction – working to make sense of the sentence – rather than as a result of the writer's clear expression.

(2) (a) Version 2 is most clearly expressed.

(b) Television talent shows can create new stars very quickly. <u>They</u> give instant exposure to an enormous audience. As a result, <u>they</u> can become famous overnight.

(c) Television talent shows can create new stars very quickly. <u>These programmes</u> give instant exposure to an enormous audience. As a result, <u>the contestants</u> can become famous overnight.

(3) (a) My hands shook as I held the envelope and I remembered my wish from the night before. <u>It</u> was small and brown but it might change my life. <u>They</u> fumbled as I clumsily tore <u>it</u> open.

(b) My hands shook as I held the envelope and I remembered my wish from the night before. <u>This envelope</u> was small and brown but it might change my life. <u>My fingers</u> fumbled as I clumsily tore <u>the letter</u> open.

## Page 38

Example

(1) My mum bought me a hamster when I started secondary school. She bought me an amazing cage to keep **him** in, full of runs and tunnels and secret hideaways. I called **my little furry friend** Billy. I loved that little **creature**.

One day, I woke up and went to see **Billy**. I looked in the cage. **It** was empty. I **peered** behind the cage. I **hunted** all over my room. I **searched** all over the house. **Billy** was gone. I was so upset I didn't know what to do. That was when I made my wish. I wished that **my hamster** would come home.

# Unit 6

## Page 43

(1) (a) For example:

i. Social media is great because you can chat to friends wherever they are, but it can also cause problems.

ii. Although social media is great and you can chat to your friends wherever they are, it can also cause problems.

iii. When you chat to your friends wherever they are, social media is great but it can also cause problems.

## Page 44

(1) (a) S: Teenagers; V: are.

(b) S: It V: was.

(c) S: I V: wanted.

(2) The second version is the most clearly expressed. The subject–verb start and the position of the adverbial 'for a whole day' provide greater clarity.

(3) (a) Many adults think that teenagers live fun and carefree lives. They could not be more wrong. Teenagers actually live their lives under constant pressure.

**(b)** The version with three sentences is expressed more clearly. However, linking two of the clauses with a conjunction might be equally clear but more fluent. Sentence structure should be an active choice depending on the intended impact of the writing.

## Page 45

**(1)** **(a)** (i) and (iii) are correct.

**(b)** (ii) is incorrect because the two clauses are linked with a comma and should be either separated by a full stop or linked with a conjunction.

**(2)** **(a)** (ii), (iii) and (iv) are correct.

**(b)** (i) is incorrect because the two clauses are linked with a comma and should be either separated by a full stop or linked with a conjunction.

**(3)** When adults see teenagers standing around the high street, they think we're doing nothing. They don't understand the pressure we're under. Friends, exams, homework, the future and even fashion are all big worries for teenagers.

## Page 46

For example:

I was beginning to lose my temper. Then I had a really stupid idea. I decided we should make a cake. I found a recipe book and got the flour, eggs, butter and sugar out of the cupboard. While I was turning on the oven, George dropped two eggs on the floor. While I was trying to find a cloth, George decided it would be easier to make the cake on the floor and started tipping flour and sugar on top of the broken eggs. That was when Mum came home. She started screaming.

# Unit 7

## Page 50

- Both texts use short sentences and paragraphs to achieve additional emphasis.

- The Paper 1 response uses series of coordinate clauses to provide a cumulative image of the theme park: 'Roundabouts and waltzers... huge wheels... tiny people...'

- The Paper 1 response uses a developed single clause sentence filled with listed details of 'shouts... screams... laughter...' etc., to similar effect.

- The Paper 2 response positions three coordinate clauses in a triple pattern in its final sentence to create impact: '...turn it off, go outside and get moving.'

## Page 51

**(1)** **(a)**
- The first sentence is the topic sentence, introducing the key point about the quantity of television programmes available: 'The quantity of television you could watch...'
- This is supported with evidence: 'Hundreds of channels...'
- The remaining sentences contrast and develop this point, building to a 'call to action': 'Switch it off instead.'

**(b)** Both the final and penultimate sentences could be positioned in their own short paragraph, either together or separately.

**(2)** For example:

The roller coaster cars began to climb. We climbed higher and higher. My pulse was racing as the people below got smaller and smaller. Higher and still higher we climbed. I closed my eyes and listened to the blood pounding in my ears. We slowed down and I knew we had nearly reached the top. And then everything disappeared and we soared down into the darkness.

I screamed and screamed until it stopped.

## Page 52

**(1)** **(a)** Through the night, as we approached the park, echoed thumping music and screams.

**(b)** All are arguable.

**(2)** **(a)** For example:
- We will, in the future, get all our information and entertainment from the internet. Televisions will become extinct like the dinosaurs.
- Like dinosaurs, televisions will become extinct in the future. We will get all our information and entertainment from the internet.

## Page 53

**(1)** **(a)** Dashes, ellipses and exclamation marks added.

**(b)** All are arguable. However, the ellipsis in Version 1 is, perhaps, less appropriate or effective than the single dash in Version 2.

**(c)**
- Exclamation marks can add emphasis or suggest the use of humour, although tend to be overused.
- Single and double dashes can be used parenthetically to add emphasis by creating a 'pause'.
- Ellipses can be used to create a pause, often to suggest something unsaid but implied.

**(2)** For example:
- Nothing, absolutely nothing, could have prepared me for that ride – I was terrified!
- Nothing – absolutely nothing! – could have prepared me for that ride... I was terrified.

## Page 54

**(1)** For example:

Some people think that television can have a big influence on our lives. They say that we will copy crime or violence if we see in television programmes. Some children's programmes have, for example, been banned or edited to remove violence. Yet even very young children can tell the difference between fiction and reality. Adults certainly can. Television should show the world as it really is - and that means showing crime and violence.

You can easily turn the television off if you don't want to see what is being shown.

# Unit 8

## Page 59

(1) Version A is most appropriate. Version B is excessively wordy and formal; Version C is too informal.

(2) He was staring at me and I wondered what he was looking at. He said, 'Need some help, mate?' I replied, 'Maybe, yeah.'

Note that an informal register is acceptable in narrative dialogue.

## Page 60

(1) For example, bland and boring.

(3) For example, I tripped and smashed my head into the pavement. It was agony.

## Page 61

(1) Version B is more precise and concise and, in part because of that concision, more vivid. Overuse of modification can dilute a sentence's impact.

(2) For example: Salad is delicious.

Note that some of the adjective choices contribute significantly to the writer's opinion, e.g. *crisp*, *juicy*, *succulent*, *fresh*, *healthy*. However, it is important to strike a balance between concision and precision when selecting vocabulary for specific effect.

# Unit 9

## Page 66

(1) The Paper 1 response demonstrates a significant range of vocabulary selected for impact. The Paper 2 response is clearly expressed, but its impact could be greatly increased with more effective vocabulary choices.

## Page 67

(1) (a) For example, affect > harm > damage > crush > shatter > destroy >annihilate

(b) Although all are arguable, it could be argued that 'affect', 'harm' and 'damage' are weak whereas 'annihilate' is overly dramatic.

## Page 68

(1) A ii. contains, range.

B i. bombards, unnecessary, unreliable.

C iii. allows, access, wealth, useful, valuable.

(2) A creates a positive, inviting tone: wandered, grass, wildflowers, ramshackle, cottage, looking, elderly, smiling. B creates a more disturbing, menacing tone: stumbled, weeds, brambles, crumbling, ruin, lurking, old, smirking.

## Page 69

(1) (a) big, mistake, really, upset.

mistake: error, blunder.

really: desperately, terribly, utterly.

upset: distraught, hysterical, devastated.

Published by Pearson Education Limited, 80 Strand, London, WC2R 0RL.

www.pearsonschoolsandfecolleges.co.uk

Text © Pearson Education Limited 2016
Produced and typeset by Tech-Set Ltd, Gateshead
Original illustrations © Pearson Education Ltd 2016

The right of David Grant to be identified as author of this work has been asserted by him in accordance with the Copyright, Designs and Patents Act 1988.

First published 2016

19 18 17 16
10 9 8 7 6 5 4 3 2 1

**British Library Cataloguing in Publication Data**
A catalogue record for this book is available from the British Library

ISBN 978 0435 18329 5

**Copyright notice**
All rights reserved. No part of this publication may be reproduced in any form or by any means (including photocopying or storing it in any medium by electronic means and whether or not transiently or incidentally to some other use of this publication) without the written permission of the copyright owner, except in accordance with the provisions of the Copyright, Designs and Patents Act 1988 or under the terms of a licence issued by the Copyright Licensing Agency, Barnards Inn, 86 Fetter Lane, London EC4A 1EN(www.cla.co.uk). Applications for the copyright owner's written permission should be addressed to the publisher.

Printed in Slovakia by Neografia

**Acknowledgements**
The publisher would like to thank the following for their kind permission to reproduce their photographs:

(Key: b-bottom; c-centre; l-left; r-right; t-top)

**Pearson Education Ltd**: Miguel Domínguez Muñoz 1r, 3r, 6r, 7r; **Shutterstock.com**: Lucky Business 1l, 3l, 6l, 7l
All other images © Pearson Education